Pradeep Bhandari, an Indian journalist and psephologist of repute, is the consulting editor of Zee Media Network. He is founder and editor-in-chief of Jan Ki Baat, a psephological and data platform which predicts results of elections through a unique and indigenously developed data-crunching model. Since 2016, Pradeep has traversed 400 Lok Sabha constituencies, almost one lakh kilometre, and predicted more than 40 Indian elections with precision. He has a proven accuracy record of 98 per cent. In the past, he has also been the consulting editor with Republic Media Network and news director with India News.

Praise for the Book

'I rarely comment on politics. But that doesn't mean I'm not interested in it! And for those Indians who are interested in how politics and elections play out in our country, one of the best things to do is to read Pradeep's analysis. He has written this book after visiting 400 Lok Sabha constituencies and travelling one lakh km through 25 states.

Modi 3.0: Bigger, Higher, Stronger is a fascinating and insightful book.

— **Amish Tripathi**,
Bestselling author and former diplomat

'A remarkable journey has produced a remarkable book. While Pradeep has always been forthright in his analysis, particularly psephological, he takes all his skills that he has honed over the past decade to another level in this book. Invigorating and informative at the same time, this is a must-read.'

— **Anand Ranganathan**,
Author and scientist

'The electoral dynamics of India is now of global interest and there are many ways to delve into it—crunching data from past elections, academic analysis of social dynamics, conducting ever larger opinion polls or, as Pradeep Bhandari does it, diving into the ocean. This is India's electoral story as told by someone who has immersed himself for years in the rough and tumble of electioneering on the ground.'

— **Sanjeev Sanyal**,
Writer and economist

'Pradeep Bhandari is an intrepid psephologist and a journalist who bases his conclusions on conversations with real and ordinary people on the ground. Fiercely independent, he has shaken up the world of stodgy reporting with his blunt assessments. His is a serious voice of the new, self-confident Bharat.'

— **Swapan Dasgupta,**
Political writer

'This book is essentially about how India will become a great nation through the 2024 electoral route. It helps us understand the factors that will play a major role in the expected NDA's win. Coming from the pen of one who has covered electoral politics and its intricacies as a psephologist from close quarters it makes an interesting and authentic reading.

Congratulations, Pradeep Bhandari, for an engrossing work!'

— **Uday Mahurkar,**
Eminent author and thinker,
Former Central Information Commissioner

'Dive into the heart of Indian politics with *Modi 3.0* by Pradeep Bhandari, a groundbreaking exploration of India's unique political landscape. With meticulous attention to detail and unparalleled access to ground-level sentiments, Bhandari delivers a compelling analysis of the 2014 and 2019 elections, paving the way for a bold prediction for the upcoming 2024 Lok Sabha Elections. Through extensive travel and data collection across India, Bhandari provides readers with unparalleled insights, steering clear of political biases to present a refreshing perspective driven solely by the voice of the people. This book, much like its author, Pradeep Bhandari, is infused with real energy, making it dynamic, vibrant and energetic—much like the ever-evolving landscape of Indian politics.'

— **Vivek Ranjan Agnihotri**,
National Award-winning Filmmaker

MODI 3.0

BIGGER, HIGHER, STRONGER

PRADEEP BHANDARI

Om Books International

First published in 2024 by

Om Books International

Corporate & Editorial Office
A-12, Sector 64, Noida 201 301
Uttar Pradesh, India
Phone: +91 120 477 4100
Email: editorial@ombooks.com
Website: www.ombooksinternational.com

Sales Office
107, Ansari Road, Darya Ganj,
New Delhi 110 002, India
Phone: +91 11 4000 9000
Email: sales@ombooks.com
Website: www.ombooks.com

ISBN: 978-81-19750-32-0

Printed in India

10 9 8 7 6 5 4 3 2 1

To my parents who are
my biggest strength and inspiration

Contents

Foreword

Prime Minister Narendra Modi's 10-year leadership of India has totally transformed the nation. He has successfully tackled the biggest challenge India has had—the poverty and deprivation of the majority of its citizens. As we go to the polls in 2024 for Modi 3.0, he has ensured that almost all Indians have a roof over their head, water in the tap, power in the switch, a gas stove at home, a toilet at home, food on the table, a bank account, money in the bank, a mobile phone, an internet connection, a road to the house, and health insurance with a contributory accident and pension policy! Never before has any PM been able to deliver all this on this scale even though all of them had good schemes and promised to reduce poverty. Poverty is at an all-time low.

Economic growth has grown from around ₹1131 crore of GDP to about ₹2,94l crore over 10 years. Reforms such as GST, the bankruptcy code, PLI, *aatmanirbhar* in defence, reduction of corporate tax to accelerate investment, have been impactful. Huge number of new jobs have been created due to economic growth as evidenced in the over seven crore new enrolments in the EPFO and ESI schemes. Our banking systems has been cleansed of political interference and high bad debts. Infrastructure investment in railways, roadways, power, including green power, etc., are at all all-time high. All remote and neglected parts of India have seen growth. All this with no corruption in the government at Delhi!

He has also increased the visibility and respect for India overseas, protected our borders against terrorism and encroachment. The G20 meet in India, and India being the fifth-largest economy on its way to become the third-largest by 2027, augurs well for us. Indians, particularly India's youth, are optimistic and upbeat about our future.

As we go to the polls in 2024, the Big Question is about Modi 3.0 and the next five years. Is he coming back to power, what are the number of seats he may get, which states, etc., are the key questions citizens are asking. Pradeep Bhandari, in this new book, seeks to answer all this based on his extensive travel and psephological analysis on the ground. His deep insights over the last eight years, travelling more than one lakh km across the length and breadth of the country as a psephologist and journalist have enabled him to understand Indian polity and the Indian voter very incisively based on deep academic research. This book is key to a greater understanding of the phenomenon of Narendra Modi—the best prime minister in India's history as a free republic—and the General Elections 2024 which will again transform India and hopefully make our future even better.

T.V. Mohandas Pai,
Chairman
Aarin Capital Partners

Introduction

'India gets ready for the celebration of democracy ... A mammoth exercise in democracy which is the world's largest electoral movement of man and material' —Election Commission of India, *Financial Express*, 16 March 2024

The year 2014 did not merely usher in a change in government, it reflected a change in public sentiment—a new political order was established. Indian polity is passing through an inflection point. The old Lutyens elite incorrectly thought that the huge mandate in support of Narendra Modi was a political aberration. Therefore, 2019 came as a shock to them. As the founder of Jan Ki Baat, I remember travelling the length and breadth of the country, tracking voter sentiment and making a bold claim of 300+ for the Bharatiya Janata Party (BJP) in the run-up to the 2019 General Elections. I had to face months of trenchant criticism for presenting the true opinion of the people of India from the ground in my previous book. Traversing one lakh km across 25 states and 400 Lok Sabha constituencies in the last eight years has culminated in this book—a political and psephological examination of the outcomes of the 2024 Lok Sabha Elections. My conclusions are based on the Jan Ki Baat's Probability Map of Outcome Model and the primary data collected by the team that polled across the length and breadth of the country from January 2024 to March 2024. For the purpose of the purity of analysis, we have kept 'people' at the focal point, strictly avoided hearsay evidence, and did not engage with any politician who could influence our observations. The team's findings documented in this book reflect the *jan ki baat* (voice of the people) on the standings of candidates and parties, and the specific issues that will have a bearing on the election. I have presented the new grammar of the current and the emerging political discourse.

This election is unique; it will see the National Democratic Alliance (NDA) under Prime Minister Narendra Modi expanding to become a bigger alliance, which I call the Super NDA, to achieve its ambitious target of winning 400 in the 18th Lok Sabha. On the other hand, the Congress party is making a last-ditch attempt to save its shrinking seat share by trying to float the rebranded *mahagathbandhan,* the Indian National Developmental Inclusive Alliance (INDIA). Our findings confirm what is already common knowledge: as far as the 2024 General Elections are concerned, the BJP remains firmly in pole position. The advantage is principally driven by Prime Minister Modi's enduring popularity.

In the first chapter, I present the sentiment on the ground in the run-up to the *prana pratishtha* (consecration) of Ram Lalla at Ram Mandir in Ayodhya on 22 January 2024.

In Chapter 2, I conduct a SWOT analysis of the NDA and the INDIA bloc based on various political factors.

In Chapter 3, I make psephological predictions of the forthcoming general elections based on the Jan Ki Baat pre-poll primary data and present conclusions by assigning probabilities to various political scenarios.

In Chapter 4, I take a deep dive into the 'Modi phenomenon', and what it means for the people of India.

In the final chapter, I discuss the way forward for Indian polity.

Writing this book was a challenging exercise for me considering the rapidly changing political scenario giving rise to various variables. However, unravelling the intricacies of the voter sentiment and trying to accurately capture the full complexity of the dynamics of the Indian general election are exciting and exhilarating to say the least. I introduce to the readers my first pre-election psephological study of the great Indian electorate.

1
Ayodhya

The Pulse of the Electorate

'If 2014 was a mandate on anti-incumbency and 2019 was a vote on delivery, 2024 is about ananda.'

You may wonder why my book on the 2024 Lok Sabha Elections begins in Ayodhya. *Well, the pulse of the voters from the majority community beats here.*

As 2023 rolled into 2024, I greeted the new year in one of the most sacred places in India, Ayodhya. The air was palpable with excitement. Every nook and corner of the city seemed to be in breathless anticipation for the much-awaited event—prana pratishtha of the idol of Ram Lalla at the Sri Ram Mandir. With the case of Ram Janmabhoomi (or the Ayodhya case), the longest-running case in Indian history, finally settled by the Supreme Court in favour of Ram Lalla, by a unanimous decision, the grand Ram Mandir was going to open its doors for a multitude of devotees after centuries of waiting. I felt blessed to be here at the cusp of such a historic moment. As I stood on the banks of the Sarayu, the psephologist and journalist in me was also excited about the upcoming elections to the 18th Lok Sabha to be held from 19 April 2024 to 1 June 2024 in seven different phases, with the results to be announced on 4 June. The world's largest democracy will be voting to return the 543 elected members of India's powerful lower house, the Lok Sabha. I was raring to go!

Votebank Politics Explained

Ayodhya was my touchstone of the political outcomes to come. Since Independence, the polity of India, dominated by the Congress and their allies—the communist parties and the Left-wing intellectuals, as is the current form of address—have been holding on to power by dividing the majority vote or the Hindu vote and consolidating the minority vote or the Muslim vote. They were convinced that Hindus could never unite on any issue and hence the Hindu consciousness was not something they needed to address. As they continue to hold this belief, they leave the gates of the Lok Sabha wide open for their nemesis. This is self-inflicted short-sightedness. Why you may ask.

Lord Ram is very dear to the followers of the Sanatan Dharma. Ram *naam* is taken by Hindus when greeting each other and chanted during last rites. Unfortunately, a section of the Indian political entity has slandered the holy chant of *Jai Shri Ram* by communalizing it. That they have got it wrong was abundantly clear as I walked through the streets of Ayodhya. Because I heard continuous chants of Jai Shri Ram, not only by devotees from the Hindi heartland, but also from those who hailed from Karnataka, Andhra Pradesh, Tamil Nadu and other parts of the country. Jai Shri Ram is the heartfelt chant of a majority of Hindus in the country.

Unfortunately, playing divisive politics has been the mainstay of the Congress and its coalition partners since

Independence and it formed the fulcrum of the policy politics of the UPA (United Progressive Alliance) era, particularly during the UPA-2 regime when it reached its peak. Many leaders of the Congress have even taken this narrative to an extreme by questioning the existence of Lord Ram and calling the existence of the Ram Setu *kalpanik*, imaginary or fictional. Former veteran Congress leader Kapil Sibal had blithely ignored the five hundred years of wait for the culmination of the Lord's case and *argued for the deferment of the hearing of the Ayodhya dispute till the completion of the 2019* Lok Sabha Elections. Despite being in power for more than 15 years, Congress leaders Sonia Gandhi and Rahul Gandhi did not think it was politically prudent to take Lord Ram's blessings at the mandir.

In stark contrast, Narendra Modi was the only prime minister who visited Ayodhya for the fifth time when he had participated in the prana pratishtha ceremony on 22 January 2024. He has laid great emphasis on embracing our ancient cultural roots and taking immense pride in the civilizational glory of Bharat.

Even prominent leaders of the INDIA bloc like Akhilesh Yadav, Mamata Banerjee, Sharad Yadav declined the invitation to attend the prana pratishtha ceremony, calling it 'an RSS and BJP event' and thus a political function.

If the Babri Masjid litigant, Iqbal Ansari, could attend the ceremony, why couldn't our leaders of the Opposition? Iqbal Ansari even encouraged people to visit Ayodhya to seek the blessings of Lord Ram ahead of the grand ceremony.

He further added that whatever may have been the struggle during the dispute, it has now ceased completely. Why has it not ended with these naysayers?

Déjà vu? Many analysts say that this stance held by the Congress is realpolitik but anyone who is a student of Indian history will remember that former Prime Minister Jawaharlal Nehru had written a letter to President Dr Rajendra Prasad advising him not to attend the inauguration ceremony of Somnath Temple years ago. The media reported that a few state Congress leaders and members of other parties disagreed with their senior leadership about boycotting the prana pratishtha of Ram Lalla at the Shri Ram Mandir. Deputy Chief Minister of Karnataka DK Shivakumar held special pujas in 34,000 state-owned temples across Karnataka to mark the occasion. 'At the end of the day, all of us are Hindus so any person connected to the ground understands that the DNA of this country is Sanatan in nature and will know what Ram Mandir means to the people of India (*Times of India*, 9 January 2024).'

Boycotting the prana pratishtha ceremony defines the Congress's modus operandi of 'secularism' that it has practised for decades. Its political philosophy, dominated by the Leftist ideology, believes that secularism is nothing but taking Hindus for granted while giving special treatment to minorities. So, the verdict of 2014 was a verdict of hope and against this politically motivated appeasement policy. The 2019 verdict was a vindication of the delivery of Prime Minister Modi's schemes, but at the same time, it was also a message given by the Hindus that they will not want to return to the era where they were treated as second-rate citizens.

Calling the Ram Lalla prana pratishtha ceremony at Ayodhya Ram Mandir a political event hurts the sentiments of many Sanatanis in India and globally. The resurgent Hindu community will unhesitatingly call out this blatant pseudo-secularism act by any political party. The leaders of the INDIA faction have shot themselves in the foot.

The Left-leaning intellectuals and politicians have done a great disservice to the Indian polity by wrongly blaming the Hindu community for communal politics. It needs to be reiterated that communal politics took birth in India when such politicians primarily focused on consolidating the Muslim vote to win elections. And that they have made a virtue of this can be seen in many policies of governments before the Modi regime. Remember the nine-second video clip of former Prime Minister Manmohan Singh which had gone viral on social media, where he said that the first right to resources in India belonged to the Muslims? It was Prime Minister Rajiv Gandhi who overturned the Supreme Court verdict in the Shah Bano case to appease the Muslim voter. Most of the members of the INDIA bloc did not support the move by the Modi government to strike off the discriminatory and unconstitutional instantaneous triple talaq.

Thus, the birth and the rise of communal politics in the country has not been because of Narendra Modi or the BJP. It arose precisely because of the votebank politics practised by the Congress and its allies. This brand of socio-political thinking dominated the political discourse of the country for over five decades, driving the narrative against Hindu sentiments. So, Hindu pride or any Hindu aspiration was termed communal by those very same people who divided and ruled through communal politics. History has a decisive way of treating such irony.

Ayodhya Is *Not* a Political Non-issue

In recent years, India has moved away from communal politics to politics of equality, wherein Sanatan Dharma as a traditional system is valued and the Hindu community is also respected and heard. *Doesn't the Constitution speak about equality for all?* Elsewhere in the world, one would be hard-pressed to find a democratic state in which the majority has had to defend its right to demand the resurrection of its most revered place of worship, among other issues. The Hindu consciousness which was subverted for many decades can no longer be ignored.

Ayodhya symbolizes the historical neglect by this power group. In the post-2014 era, the politics of neglecting the majority for the minority has become an expired cheque. Despite this, the politicians who formed the INDIA bloc in July 2023 failed to understand the prevailing sentiment. They made the same mistake in 2019 and the statements of the leaders of the alliance in the run-up to the historic consecration at the Ram Mandir indicate that they are all set to repeat the mistake in 2024. Since this group has not acknowledged the sentiments of the majority community, they never felt the need to address their demand to resurrect the destroyed temple at the birthplace of Shri Ram. Considering this desire as a political non-issue, many of these leaders have never even bothered to visit the mandir let alone supporting the building of the Ram Mandir. It was never a part of their election manifesto.

On the other hand, a majority of Hindu voters saw their sentiments being echoed in the BJP's election manifesto, and voted for it. Narendra Modi is the first Sanatani prime minister who has come to power for two successive terms with a thumping majority. It took a long time but there is no denying the fact that after the Supreme Court judgment on 9 November 2019, little time was wasted. Honouring their manifesto promise, Prime Minister Narendra Modi performed the *bhoomi pujan* at the temple site on 5 August 2020, and since then the construction of the Ram Mandir has been going on at a rapid pace. People associate the building of the temple with Modi's government and particularly with Narendra Modi himself—he has been very visible.

So, when on 22 June 2023, the Temple Construction Committee chairman Nripendra Misra announced that the ground floor of the three-storey temple was complete and was expected to open for devotees in January 2024, I landed in Ayodhya towards the end of December 2023. I had received an invitation for the prana pratishtha ceremony of Ram Lalla in the Ram Mandir on the golden letter day of 22 January 2024. The journalist in me smelt something big was going to happen. The *bhakt* in me was humbled and eager to have the *darshan* of Prabhu Sri Ram at the Ram Mandir.

Ayodhya is very special to me. When the Supreme Court delivered its judgment by *sarv sammati*, unanimously, in 2019 in favour of Ram Lalla, I was there. When Prime Minister Modi performed the bhoomi pujan, I was there. Hence, I felt extremely fortunate to be in Ayodhya in the run-up to the prana pratishtha ceremony that most Hindus have been waiting for the last 500 years. And now I had received an invitation for the prana pratishtha ceremony at the Ram Mandir! On this historic day, I would be in Ayodhya.

I felt buoyed by the bustling energy around me and felt very privileged to be there. Ayodhya was milling with pilgrims and tourists from across the country and the world. What was on their mind and that of the residents of Ayodhya? I was eager to know about the prevailing political sentiment and the issues that the people were grappling with.

Yogi Adityanath's government, under the aegis of Prime Minister Modi, has developed four main paths—Bhakti Path, Ramjanmabhoomi Path, Ram Path and Dharma Path in Ayodhya, epitomizing a blend of tradition and modernity.

The Bhakti Path is a modern pathway that leads to the Ram Mandir. It is a 500-metre stretch, flanked with greenery that offers shade to pilgrims who come to the Ram Mandir from all over the country and the world. There are benches, seating facilities and counters where assistance is provided to the differently abled. There is also a facility for prasad collection and donation.

It is to be noted that neither the state government nor the Central government has given money for the construction of the Ram Mandir. The Shri Ram Janmabhoomi Teerth Kshetra Trust was formed by the Central government in February 2020 to handle the construction and maintenance of the Ram Mandir. The trust has received more than ₹3,000 crore from approximately four lakh villages across the country due to the effort of the Rashtriya Swayamsevak Sangh (RSS). That is why Ram Mandir is also called Bharat's mandir.

Ram Mandir: Uniting the Nation

As I started walking up the stretch, I noticed hundreds of people disembarking from several buses and walking along Bhakti Path. They were from the Kashi Tamil Sangamam. Initiated by Prime Minister Modi to reaffirm and re-establish the age-old ties between Tamil Nadu and Kashi, they were now arriving in busloads from Tamil Nadu to Ayodhya for Ram darshan. Their ties were with Kashi, so how did the Ram Mandir hold any place in their heart? As I tried to look for an answer to the question that arose in my mind, I fell in step with Silva and got clarity the moment we started talking. He was well aware of the political and legal struggle to reclaim Ram Janmabhoomi, and he was in Ayodhya to rejoice in the building of the Ram Mandir in the lord's birthplace. The passion with which he responded gave me goosebumps. But he was not the only one.

I soon caught up with another group from Tamil Nadu and asked them about their feelings as they walked up this path to visit the temple. A gentleman in his sixties spoke on their behalf and said, 'We are very fortunate to visit Ayodhya and have darshan of Prabhu Shri Ram, our God. We are very grateful to the prime minister for making our dream come true.'

Such sentiments were not limited to the citizens of Ayodhya or the people of the Hindi heartland, as some may have you believe. They cut across geography, caste and even demography. I was overwhelmed because anyone in touch with news from Tamil Nadu will know about the rather offensive statements by Tamil Nadu Sports Minister and Dravida Munnetra Kazhagam (DMK) scion Udhayanidhi Stalin against Sanatan Dharma at the Sanatana Abolition Conference in September 2023. As the party has won a majority, one can be forgiven for thinking that Tamilians were okay with such expressions that callously hurt the sentiment of the Hindus. But then here were devout Tamilians walking the streets of Ayodhya in deep reverence of Lord Ram and taking great pride in the Ram Mandir.

A group of youngsters in their late teens were also walking on the Bhakti Path and greeted me with chants of Jai Shri

Ram, Jai Shri Ram. They were from Sitamarhi, Bihar. They told me that they were joyous that the Ram Mandir was being built and that five hundred years ago, our ancestors would not have been able to believe that such a miracle could occur. Having taken darshan of the deity, they were filled with joy, *sammaan* (pride) and at the same time felt great *santushthi* (contentment).

I asked them, 'Do you think this temple would have been built if Modi's government had not come to power?'

One of them stated categorically, 'No, if it wasn't for Modiji, Ram Mandir wouldn't have been built. Modiji has done something that no other prime minister could do, and we will remember him for the rest of our lives. We pray to Ishwar that Shri Narendra Modi remains the prime minister of our country.'

The others in the group vigorously nodded their heads in unison.

It became obvious to me that Narendra Modi had been able to successfully gauge the aspirations and desires of the majority of citizens. It seems they had finally found a political leader who could understand their needs, and was one of them. And then I recalled my travels through many constituencies in the run-up to the 2019 Lok Sabha Elections. It was abundantly clear then that the voter sentiment was favouring the reinstatement of Narendra Modi as the prime minister, and that he would return to power with huge numbers. This time, I got the feeling that the voter sentiment was *even more* inclined towards Prime Minister Modi.

I had by now almost reached the Ram Mandir for darshan of Shri Ram. The darshan would be given elsewhere, as the newly built Ram Mandir was set to open to the public after the prana pratishtha. Here, I met a few old ladies—some of them were in wheelchairs. They were from Jhajjar and Rohtak in Haryana. I asked them how they felt on being able to take darshan at the Ram Mandir. They answered that they felt as if they were living a fantasy because they could never imagine that they would be able to do so. One of them said, 'Now, I can die in peace because I have been able to behold my Prabhu.'

As these sentiments reverberated with each conversation, I was overwhelmed by the magnitude of goodwill for the prime minister. My research over the years has convinced me that Narendra Modi has been able to touch the hearts and minds of a wide cross-section of Indians.

Understanding the Temple Economy

After the darshan, I walked back down the Bhakti Path towards the serene Sarayu that flows by the holy city. Faith has it that it flows from the big toe of the left foot of Lord Vishnu and it was on its banks that Shri Ram had taken his *samadhi*. Thus, it holds a special place in the hearts of the Hindus and has great significance for them. The bridge near the Sarayu bears witness to a stampede triggered by firing on the *karsevak*s when they were trying to enter Ayodhya at the peak of the Ram Janmabhoomi movement in the 1990s.

When I spoke to people near Sarayu Ghat, they pointed out with great pride at how clean the ghat was, how clean the river was and that before 2014 nobody bothered about how polluted the river was. It was like a nullah, full of contaminated water; no one even cared to know if the Sarayu was flowing. But a change in the government changed all that. Look how beautifully it is cared for now.

The river did look inviting, so I paid a boatman ₹400 and stepped into his boat. As he steered the boat across the gentle Sarayu, I asked Radhey Sham how he felt about the Ram Mandir being built in Ayodhya.

He responded, 'Bhai, I am feeling very happy, and my entire *parivar* is waiting to pay homage when the mandir opens for *aam janta*.' I asked him how his business was faring, and he said something important that must be understood.

He said, 'The Ram Mandir is drawing so many bhakts now, even though the prana pratishtha rituals are yet to be performed. My economic condition has improved as more and more bhakts and tourists have started pouring in. Today I am earning a minimum of ₹400 per day in comparison to only ₹100 to ₹150 earlier. Since Modiji's government has come to power, the city's infrastructure has improved immensely and as a result, many more tourists are visiting Ayodhya. When the Ram Mandir will open, we will be covered in silver, that is, earn even more. We will be able to earn money the way people do in Kashi.'

I had spent many days walking on the streets of Ayodhya and interviewing Ayodhya *niwasis*. Towards the end of my visit, I pondered over the surge of sentiment that was driving the election. Surely this is not just about spirituality, this is just not about Sanatan revivalism, this is also about economics. It was around this time, I viewed a video of Nripendra Misra, the officer architect of the Ram Mandir, informing the viewers that with the construction of Ram Mandir, there will be on average one to three lakh tourists visiting Ayodhya daily.

The increase in footfall will certainly have a ripple effect on the local as well as the state economy. As Prime Minister Modi puts it, the mandir stands both for *vikas*, progress in terms of revenue generation and employment, and *virasat*, heritage and tradition. Ayodhya anticipates an infusion of funds to the tune of over ₹8,500 crore, which will transform it into a global tourism destination (*Times of India,* 10 January 2024). The Master Plan for the city includes a new township spread over 1,200 acres, which can host over three lakh visitors—both domestic and international—per day.

The Ayodhya airport, officially called Maharishi Valmiki International Airport, opened on 30 December 2023, and the revamped railway station (or Ayodhya Dham) will attract not only millions of bhakts, but also people drawn to disciplines like yoga and meditation. Ayodhya will become a global hub of spiritual and heritage tourism. It is needless to say that the influx of investment and tourism will generate thousands of jobs across several sectors, especially in the tourism and hospitality industry.

In Ayodhya, the hotel industry is already booming with the advent of big hotel chains like the Taj, the Leela. The local daily-wage earners are looking forward to a rise in their earnings with the great inpouring of visitors to their city. People are renting out their houses for homestays and bed and breakfasts. There is the absolute belief that Ayodhya will become a world tourism hub. They are even expecting that in the years to come, they will have to extend Ayodhya like they had to extend New Delhi. Thus, the entire economy of the region is poised to be transformed. I will discuss in detail the impact of Prime Minister Modi's policies and governance later in this book.

Historically, the Hindu communities always had economies built around temples which allowed local residents to find a deeper meaning to life by connecting with God. But at the same time, it also fuelled the local economy. Unfortunately, as mentioned earlier, our political masters since Independence have mostly had a very Western way of looking at development. They did not focus on building temple economies. As already mentioned, Prime Minister Modi is the first Sanatani prime minister who has grassroots connections and performed service at the ground level for the past 40 years. Therefore, he has a very organic understanding of the issues that are important to the masses and hence has focused on building temple economies.

Kashi has been transformed after the cleaning of its ghats, and now sees more tourists than Goa. Ayodhya is getting transformed ever since the construction of the Ram Mandir began, and a similar transformation has occurred at the Mahakaleshwar Temple in Ujjain, and even in Anantnag district of South Kashmir with the re-opening of the Martand Surya Temple in Mattan.

The Modi Tripod

So, why do people support the prime minister? Prime Minister Modi's charisma hinges on three factors. I call this the Modi Tripod.

Establishing Civilizational Renaissance and Sanatan Pride

Strongly developed nations are those who learn from their past and remain rooted in their culture. After gaining Independence, our leaders did not stray far from the legacy of governance left to us by the colonists. Our earlier prime ministers, particularly those of the Congress and the UPA, tried to run the country on a more Western model that undermined our thought, cultures and traditions. Prime

Minister Modi, on the other hand, knows the importance of cultural nationalism. His government is actively bringing to the fore those pages of our past that were systematically besmudged and obfuscated by colonialism and then by the Left-leaning polity that followed.

Sanatan pride is about acknowledging and celebrating our glorious cultural heritage. It forms the DNA of this country. Despite Kashi being the cradle of Sanatan Dharma, the Kashi Vishwanath Temple was grossly neglected post-Independence just like it was during the British Raj. As an old saying in the Hindi belt goes, '*Kashi ke kankar Shankar samaan* (each pebble in Kashi is as sacred as Shiva).'

Under Prime Minister Modi, the ghats of Varanasi got cleaned and the Kashi Vishwanath Temple got renovated, which has resulted in a five-fold increase in the footfall of the pilgrims. None of this could have been possible were it not for the leadership of Prime Minister Modi. He is the first prime minister who proudly projects his identity as a Sanatani. All other prime ministers of this country used to think twice before adorning the saffron attire or for that matter visiting Ayodhya. Prime Minister Modi is the one prime minister who has visited Ayodhya the maximum number of times.

Consider, for example, Priyanka Gandhi Vadra who only emerges during an election campaign and yet is considered a high-ranking Congress leader. She takes great pride in articulating that she comes from a family which has given 'so many prime ministers to this country'. There is a video of her canvassing in Ayodhya in 2019, where she was asked why she did not visit the Ram Mandir and she replied, 'Because the matter is sub judice.' What she does not realize is that people did not care that she had not visited the temple, but they did care that she had not raised the question as to why Lord Ram continued to be housed in a tent. It is this uncaring attitude that really hurt the sentiments of most Hindu voters.

The disconnect that they face from the Gandhi family is not something they experience with Prime Minister Modi. He has never hesitated to say Jai Shri Ram or and Jai Mahakal. He does not have an issue with wearing a tilak or performing an aarti at any temple. During the inauguration of the Kashi Vishwanath corridor, he said, '*Yeh sarkar Baba ka sarkar hain.*' Prime Minister Modi is a man proud of his culture.

Implementing Welfarism for People at the Bottom of the Pyramid

The second biggest reason responsible for the prime minister's incredible popularity and success is that he works to ensure overall economic development by improving the standard of living of the people at the bottom of the pyramid. When I travelled through the interiors of the country, I noticed that a huge section of the poor has benefitted from Prime Minister Modi's beneficiary schemes. Many politicians such as P. Chidambaram have claimed that these policies were initiated by the Congress and repackaged by the BJP. *But what about the implementation?* Remember Prime Minister Rajiv Gandhi's famous remark in 1985? He has gone on record to say that only 15 paise of every rupee meant for the welfare of the downtrodden reaches them.

Under the current dispensation, the beneficiaries get the entire amount. The current government under the dynamic leadership of Prime Minister Modi has ensured that whenever the indigent needed the government, it was there for them, whether it was ensuring more than 200 crore vaccine doses or providing free ration to 80 crore people during the pandemic. And the Union Cabinet has extended the free ration scheme Pradhan Mantri Garib Kalyan Anna Yojana (PMGKAY) with effect from 1 January 2024.

As per the latest data, more than around 103 crore people are dependent on direct benefit transfer (DBT) schemes of the Central government. The DBT scheme was introduced to streamline the transfer of government-provided subsidies in India. As of 11 March 2024, the government has disbursed a whopping ₹8.22 lakh crore—close to 60 per cent of the welfare and subsidies budget of the Union government—directly to the bank accounts of beneficiaries (National Informatics Centre). Facts like these are telling—whether it is providing millions of gas cylinders to BPL women who have been cooking on chulahs all their lives or ensuring that tap water reaches the households in villages through the prime minister's Har Ghar Jal scheme. As of 4 February 2024, out of 19.27 crore rural households in the country, more than

14.24 crore (73.93 per cent) households are reported to have tap water supply in their homes (Press Information Bureau, 8 February 2024). During the period (2014–2019) from the launch of Swachh Bharat Mission, more than 10 crore individual household latrines (IHHLs) were built across all states/Union Territories (UTs), and as of 2 October 2019, all states/UTs had self-reported themselves open defecation free (Press Information Bureau, 16 March 2023). The PM Vishwakarma Scheme offers support and empowerment to artisans and craftspeople across India. Roads have been constructed at the fastest pace possible in the last 20 years.

The aforementioned schemes reflect the present government's determined endeavour to improve the life of the needy by relying on two important principles—providing dignity to the poor and standing in support of the poor, in their *sukh* and *dukh* (happiness and sorrow). And then the electronic voting machines (EVMs) are blamed by the shortsighted.

Reclaiming India's Global Prestige And Pride

It cannot be argued that India's global prestige has reached an all-time high under Prime Minister Modi. The country has moved from the position of a balancing power to that of a leading power. It can purchase oil from Russia at a discounted rate and at the same time negotiate a defence deal with the USA. India has managed to retaliate acts of terrorism through punitive surgical strikes and get back then Wing Commander Abhinandan through diplomatic channels. The Global South has welcomed India acting as its spokesperson as it reaches out to fulfil the needs of its poorest members.

Indians across strata are enjoying the country's growing global influence. Let me recount an interaction I had with Shyam, an auto driver, who took me to my gym just after the G20 Summit in New Delhi. As we passed by the Bharat Mandapam, the world-class convention centre located at Pragati Maidan, I remarked, 'Bhaiya, G20 is finished, any thoughts about this?'

He replied, 'Bhaiya, I liked it very much, it showed how respected our country is, Modiji has done it.'

'But the Opposition is saying that we have spent so much money on hosting it and it was only for Modiji's publicity.'

'These guys are foolish and don't understand. If so many of the world's leaders come to Bharat and then go home safely, this shows that our respect is increasing worldwide. If Modiji was not there, we couldn't have imagined that so many leaders from so many big nations would come here. With this, our *maan-sammaan* (respect) has increased immensely. Bhaiya, earlier we would see our PM humbly go to America or the UK or China and not talk as equals. But our Modiji walks ahead of them. The American president wants to speak to him and the PM of the UK is also eager to talk with him. And today Bharat is safe from China and Pakistan because of Modiji.'

'But why spend so much money?'

'Bhaiya, tell me one thing, if a guest comes to your home, would you not feed them good food? You won't decorate your house well? This is our culture. We treat our guest like God.'

Atithi devo bhava. Narendra Modi understands this sentiment of the people because he is a man of the people.

Narendra Modi has proven to the world that not only can Bharat protect its civilizational strength and pride, but also be one of the fastest-growing economies in the world. Civilization culture and economic development go hand in hand, they are not antithesis of each other. India is churning one success story after another. Whether it is utilizing UPI payment systems or building world-class infrastructure for the nation. These now go hand in hand with ensuring that our temples, a part of our civilizational heritage, are given due respect.

Ayodhya is a model case because it represents three key aspects of Prime Minister Modi's idea of development—civilizational renaissance, rapid development and improving India's position globally. One must recognize how the policies of this government have improved the lives of the people. In 2014, there were 50 federal government schemes, which were related to the direct transfer of payments to the beneficiaries. After 2014, these have increased to more than a thousand in number. The DBT scheme aids simpler and faster flow of information and funds to the beneficiaries and reduces the chances of fraud in the delivery system. These schemes are highly inclusive in nature with the primary objective of raising people from poverty irrespective of their caste, creed or religion. Although the scheme was launched on 1 January 2013, the Modi government has done a brilliant job of expanding and implementing it. It is because Prime Minister Modi has ensured direct delivery to the poor and the marginalized without any middlemen, he is yards ahead in the race. And hence we can predict another wave, or perhaps a tsunami! It is possible. Our predictions for the 2024 General Elections have all the backing based on data and in-depth research.

'He (Modi) Is Our *Bhaijaan*'

These thoughts are firmly in my mind as my team and I gear up to gather data. The ground reality is certainly not reflecting the narrative that has been spun largely by a group of Left-leaning intellectuals in the media. Their chief argument remains: 'Oh, it is just the Hindu community that has been impacted. What about the Muslims?'

To find if this was reflected on the ground, I went to the Muslim-dominated Sutharthiya Mohalla in Ayodhya. I was anticipating dissenting and unhappy voices but I was very surprised with the outcomes of my survey. I asked a gentleman called Akhtar, 'Miyan, are you unhappy now that the temple has been built?'

He responded, 'Why would we be sad, bhai? The building of the mandir is a very good thing. Our community will get employment. Ayodhya will get developed, the city is being built up and roads are being improved. Many more tourists are going to come. We will get employment; our children will get employment. So, it's great that the legal case has been solved and the mandir has been made.'

When I told him that Asaduddin Owaisi and other politicians have said that the Muslim community is very upset about this, he replied, 'That is politicking. Why bother about them? Ask us if we are upset and then give the true picture. And why should we be upset? Now our land prices have shot up. We are being offered anything from ₹50 lakh to 2 crore and above. We could never have dreamt of having so much. We have greatly benefitted.'

Then he invited me to eat biryani at his home.

James Carville had rightly said, 'It's the economy, stupid!'

As with all communities in the country, the Muslims too want economic development. They too want the economic upliftment but have been hitherto shackled. Who kept them chained? The radical maulvis' focus has never been the economy or the upliftment of their brethren. A majority of the Muslims have realized that now. Hence, Prime Minister Modi's unbiased policies are being appreciated by those Muslims seeking a better life. Anybody who is at the bottom of the pyramid will get the benefit. And slowly this understanding is spreading across the Muslim community; however, whether or not this will translate into votes needs to be seen. But to claim that *all* Muslims are unhappy because of the construction of Ram Mandir is an inaccurate narrative.

Recently, Prime Minister Modi's minority outreach drew praise from Muslim women. When Prime Narendra Modi delivered his Mann Ki Baat address on 31 December 2023, a Muslim woman who had tuned in to listen said, 'No other party or government did as much for us as this government … PM Modi has done a lot for us. He is our *bhaijaan* (ANI, 31 December 2023).'

She added that they are now able to perform Hajj and hailed him for abolishing triple talaq while ensuring other benefits for their welfare. India tweaked its Hajj policy after Saudi Arabia allowed women's participation without a *mahram*. With these kinds of voices emanating from the Muslim community, albeit in a smaller number, the tight grip of the maulvis on the Muslim voters is loosening. Thus, it can be said that Narendra Modi as a Sanatani prime minister is not only transforming sacred religious places dear to our Sanatan faith, but also giving equal treatment to the minority community.

At one end of the spectrum are the members of the INDIA bloc who are frustrated, shocked and bewildered to see the grand Ram Mandir being built in Ayodhya. On the other, you have the people of the country, who are rejoicing at the fulfilment of a deeply held wish for the resurrection of the Ram Mandir on Ram Janmabhoomi. They are also hopeful and excited about economic upliftment that the temple will bring. Hence, the statements of leaders like Sanjay Raut saying that the country is going back 5,000 years or of the Congress leader Siddaramaiah calling the prana pratishtha ceremony at Ayodhya Ram Mandir nothing but a political gimmick, no longer resonate with the people. Such leaders are starting to lose trust and faith of the masses. No wonder their ability to garner votes has also reduced significantly. So, all these statements are those of a frustrated alliance that has cut itself off from the roots of this country.

Marmalade, Anyone?

The following imagery will help highlight the difference between Narendra Modi and leaders of the INDIA bloc. Recently, Prime Minister Modi went to Ayodhya to inaugurate a railway line and the world-class Ayodhya Airport. He then had tea with Meera Manjhi, the 10th crore beneficiary of the Ujjwala Yojana. During the course of the conversation, he was taking stock of how his schemes had impacted the lives of the beneficiaries. Were they of use to them and were they happy with the policies? He asked Meera when she got the possession of her house. Was she cooking her food on gas now? By using gas as a cooking fuel, had her health improved? Meera answered all in the affirmative. She got a house and along with it she got a gas connection and tap water. Later, he asked her family if he could be of further service to them. The prime minister wound up his visit by asking them whether they would try to work harder to enhance their lives now that they had these facilities. They cheerfully responded, 'Yes, Prime Minister, we will!' After he left, the media asked Meera what she felt about this visit. Her response said it all, 'I was thrilled that he came to meet me and my family. It is very hard to believe that our bhagwan came to visit us. I have no words to describe how happy I am.'

Narendra Modi stands for the poor, and this has been recognized by the masses. He is no longer a political leader to them, *he is family*. His connection with the masses is mutual because he has often addressed the nation as '*mere parivar jano*'. It is not a mere slogan because he is now connected to more than 100 crore people. Narendra Modi is an emotion. Narendra Modi is hope.

Now, let us draw parallels to the communication modes of Rahul Gandhi and Sonia Gandhi. They uploaded a video on 31 December 2023 where they were making marmalade, *yes marmalade*, if you please, while sending new year wishes. How many villagers would know the taste of marmalade? These leaders are totally disconnected with their Indian connection. This is why Prime Minister Modi and gets votes for his party across caste lines. He is connected with the people 24/7.

This is why I began with Ayodhya. The city has a deep connection with the populace.

2024 Will Be a Wave Election

While driving alongside the beautiful Sarayu in our car which has driven us more than one lakh km in the past eight years, I recalled predicting more than 39 Indian elections accurately. I have travelled to more than 400 Lok Sabha constituencies. My present travel schedule has brought me approximately 1,600 kilometres from home to Ayodhya.

We were shooting on the banks of the Sarayu one late night. It was about 8 or 9 degrees when a pilgrim from Gonda caught my attention. He had come for an early morning darshan and was wrapped in a blanket to ward off the cold. I noticed that he did not have fingers. I approached him and asked, 'Now that the Ram Mandir has been built in Ayodhya, what are your views on this?'

His replied, 'Modiji has made possible that which no one else has been able to do. I have lived only for this day. I will visit the temple daily in gratitude that my Prabhu Ram's mandir has been built.'

I asked, 'But the Opposition is saying that Modiji is going to lose the coming election.'

He responded, 'Nobody can defeat Modiji. He has raised the maan sammaan of this desh. I am content and ask for nothing more from him. I will pray every day to Bhagwan for his well-being.'

Such sentiments echoed in a multitude of voices interviewed by us.

My Ayodhya experience tells me that 2024 will be a wave election. Prime Minister Modi's vote share will increase, and he will return with an absolute majority without any need for alliance support. Previously, the BJP cadre canvassed on his behalf. For 2024, you have a situation where it is the people of the country who have become his campaigners, his *karyakartas*, his supporters, and they feel duty-bound to ensure that Prime Minister Modi is voted back to power with a resounding majority. This creates a recipe for a wave election. And I will not be surprised if he comes back in 2024 with a higher vote share than in 2019.

The BJP added 6.4 per cent to its 2014 vote share, taking it to 37.4 per cent, and is poised to perform even better in 2024. The party had spread its hold across 60 per cent of India's geography in 2019. There is a huge possibility that will increase further because the populace has become habitual to the development pace that Prime Minister Modi offers. He has delivered what no other prime minister could do in the past 70 years—constructing the grand temple at the birthplace of Shri Ram. This is not a Hindi heartland issue but resonates with every Sanatani in the country. The building of temples and the development of the cities have had a ripple effect on the economic upliftment of a large section of people.

There is a heart-to-heart connection.

How the Opposition Got Itself into a Political Chakravyuh

Since 2020, my team and I often served hot food to the *shramiks* who are constructing the Ram Mandir at Karsevak Puram. They had come from all over the country—Bengal, Jharkhand, Odisha, Tamil Nadu, Madhya Pradesh (MP), Bihar, Uttar Pradesh (UP). We have been performing this service since Prime Minister Modi performed the bhoomi puja of the mandir. Because apart from being a journalist and a psephologist, I am a Bhartiya, and any Bhartiya will feel immense pride on seeing the Ram Mandir being built. After dinner, all of them would watch *Ramayan* in the *karyashala* (workshop) near the Ashok Singhal Dwar. One day I asked a group of workers, 'How do you feel, knowing that you are contributing to building the Ram Mandir?

Vipul Sahu from Jharkhand said, 'I'm feeling great, we work all day from dawn to dusk. I am very fortunate that Bhagwan Ram has given me this opportunity. I've taken only three days off in the last two years. This is our *bhavana* (emotion) for Prabhu Shri Ram. This is our *tapasya* (penance) towards Shri Ram, and I wish the mandir is completed quickly.'

'Could any other government have performed this feat?'

'Only Modiji and nobody else could do this. He facilitated the making of Ram Mandir and has won our hearts. He will be immortalized for this.'

The same feelings were expressed by a group from Bengal. Bhim Prasad of Gorakhpur said, 'Modi and Yogi are there, therefore everything is possible.'

One day I took my team to visit Acharya Satyendra Das who is the chief priest of the Ram Mandir. This octogenarian has served as the *pujari* since Ram Lalla was housed in a tent. We went to meet him at his residence in Digambara *akhada* near Digambar Ghat. We were fortunate to receive his blessings. I took the opportunity to ask him about his views on Ram Mandir becoming a reality. He said, 'We were used to facing difficulties. Ram Lalla was in a tent. I used to go to the court because it directed that a court receiver should look after our needs, but that never happened. All my peers are now in heaven. Prabhu Shri Ram has made me survive till now because He wants to have the mandir.'

He recalled the struggle to get even basic facilities for Shri Ram from the earlier governments despite a court receiver being appointed.

'When it rained, our surroundings became muddy, no attention was paid by the government and no money was coming through puja, so it became an out-of-pocket expense. But Prabhu Ramji's puja continued. And today when people see the Ram Mandir, they can't believe their eyes!'

'If there had been another government in power would the mandir have been made?'

'So many governments have come and gone, but it was only Modiji's government that made it its goal of building

Prabhu Shri Ramji's mandir and achieved it. This is why Prabhu Shri Ram will look after him.'

So, the entire Sanatani *samaj* is blessing the man. When these kinds of emotions prevail, arithmetic takes a backseat in politics.

By rejecting the prana pratishtha of Ram Lalla in the Ram Mandir, the Opposition has embroiled itself in a political chakravyuh. The day when Sonia Gandhi, Adhir Ranjan Choudhury and Mallikarjun Kharge declined the invitation for the ceremony, by calling it 'an RSS/BJP event', I asked my cab driver, Kamran, about his opinion on the issue.

'Kamran, the Congress party and its alliance have turned down the invitation for the prana pratishtha of Prabhu Shri Ram. What do you have to say about this?'

Kamran replied, 'Look Bhaiya, whoever has *astha* (faith) and *shraddha* (respect) for Prabhu Shri Ram, will go to Ayodhya. Who doesn't, will not go.'

So, the Congress by doing so has not only shot itself in the foot, but also positioned itself as anti-Ram, and the narrative for 2024 has been set. My local travel agent, who lives between Ayodhya and Kashi, is now moving to Ayodhya.

I asked him, 'Bhaiya, why are you going to Ayodhya?'

He replied, 'Bhaiyaji, *ab sab kuch Ayodhya hain* (now everything is Ayodhya).'

Thus, by rejecting Shri Ram, the INDIA bloc has ensured 2024 could be about '*ab sub kuch Ayodhya hain*'.

Experiencing Ananda in Ayodhya

I was blessed to be able to attend the prana pratishtha ceremony at the Ram Mandir. Surreal is too limiting a word to describe what I felt in these moments. *Ananda* and fulfilment could be the right words, but again not enough to describe the soaring emotions within me. But these are very private moments.

After my darshan, I decided to stay with my team for a few more days to check whether or not the Ayodhya factor was indeed a Hindi heartland issue. The city was teeming with pilgrims, so we ventured forth in the evenings to interview people, sometimes staying out as late as 2 a.m., giving ourselves a chance to gauge the fervour of those out in the cold still awaiting their turn for a darshan. Would they be just as enthusiastic as those who had a darshan in the morning? They were indeed. Although it is wrong to call it a fervour, a more accurate description is *anand ka bhav* (a blissful feeling)—many a time the English language fails us in expressing our deepest of emotions.

We interviewed many people, and it would be safe to say that approximately 90 per cent were grateful to Prime Minister Modi for making the mandir a reality after a 500-year-long wait. As we walked along the Bhakti Path, we had the pleasure of meeting a wide range of people from different parts of the nation. I encountered a group from Malkagiri, Telangana: Vedvaratji (48 years), Ram Lingamji (63 years) and Sade Pavarji (45 years).

I asked them, 'Did you have a darshan?'

'Yes, we are feeling very blessed.'

When I asked about the role of Prime Minister Modi in ensuring this mandir was built, one of the gentlemen did a pranam in front of the camera and said, 'Prime Minister Narendra Modi *ko hamara* pranam.'

Outside the Tulsi Udhyan, we bumped into some youths; seventeen-year-old Apu was among them. He was wearing roller skates. He had skated 370 km from Vaishali in Bihar to Ayodhya! In the course of our discussion on the temple, he said, '*Joh Ram ko layien hain hum unko layenge* (those who have brought Ram we will bring them back).' At that, the other youths raised the slogan, 'Jai Shri Ram'.

Soon after we met a few middle-aged ladies from Karnataka. During the course of our conversation, they said, 'This is surreal, that we have been able to get Prabhu Shri Ram's darshan.' Near the Suryakund temple, we met a couple who had come all the way from New Jersey, USA. On being asked how they felt about having a darshan, the man replied, 'We are feeling very blessed. The idol is beautiful; in fact, I told Arun Yogiraj (the sculptor of Ram Lalla) that generations will remember him for the *seva* he has done of the Sanatan, that Ram Lalla has become more beautiful in the *garbha griha* (sanctum sanctorum).'

Two days after having been blessed with 7,500 other devotees for the prana pratishtha, I joined the common line, to observe how the common man was going for a darshan. Despite a huge number of pilgrims congregating daily for a darshan, the state government and the local administration ensured that the experience of the pilgrims remain hassle-free.

Every night the *Ramayan* was played on large screens for those waiting for their turn for a darshan. We had artists from Manipur performing on stage mesmerizing everyone with their scintillating performance. Lord Ram was connecting everyone, whether they were from the north, the northeast, the south and central India. Around 90 per cent of them gave credit to Prime Minister Modi for the mandir. Already half a million people had a darshan there in less than a week.

Guptaji, a sweetmeat seller, has been doing brisk business ever since the prana pratishtha of Lord Ram at the mandir. He told me, '*Ayodhya swarg ban gaya hain*. I never thought it could become heaven!'

Ayodhya at night was wonderful; even at midnight the streets were festooned with lights and shops were open with everyone helping each other. It truly felt as though Shri Ram had returned and Ayodhya was celebrating Diwali every night. There were *bhandaras* on every street corner, serving either *chhole chawal* or *puri sabzi*. It felt as though Shri Ram had united the entire country, and created a wave of merriment and jubilation.

If 2014 was a mandate on anti-incumbency and 2019 was a vote on delivery, 2024 is about ananda.

The liberals would have you think that the excitement felt by the Hindus would create communal disturbances and destroy the harmony of the nation, and that the Ram Mandir reflected a rural–urban divide. However, everywhere in and around Ayodhya, I saw young couples taking photos and posting them on social media. They proudly displayed Jai Shri Ram written across their foreheads. Now it is cool to openly be a Hindu. This display of unbridled pride is pan Indian regardless of the fact that you are a woman or a man living in south Mumbai or a town or a village anywhere in the country. I came across a group of youths dancing and chanting by the road. I soon discovered that someone among them was from IIT-Bombay and another from Banaras Hindu University. Shri Ram evoked a deep feeling within them and they too had come for a darshan.

In fact, recently, a photo of H.C. Verma went viral. He had come for a darshan in Ayodhya. He is a Padma Shri awardee and a professor of physics at IIT-Kanpur.

Raebareli: The Congress Bastion

After experiencing the joy and ananda of the people of India in Ayodhya, where people from all walks of life and all demographics, all age groups, men and women alike from different parts of India, came in equal numbers to take darshan of Prabhu Shri Ram, we travelled next to Raebareli where Sonia Gandhi had been undefeated till date. We travelled towards Hanuman Garhi and marvelled at the widening of the roads and improvement of the infrastructure. Now with the establishment of the mandir, everything has changed. At Raebareli, our objective was to check if '*sub kuch Ayodhya hain*' resonated in the Congress bastion.

What we found is that if Varanasi is a symbol of a modern civilizational city, receiving a developmental surplus; if Ayodhya represents Ramnagari united by Shri Ram and bhakti, and at the same time an accelerated infrastructural development, Raebareli represents a city deprived of development.

There we met Sindhuji who happily shared his views on the prana pratishtha, '*Bahut bhavya, bahut anand*, we watched it on Doordarshan, and we will go for a darshan.'

When I asked him about how things were in Raebareli, he replied, 'Bhaiya, there is no development, Congress might have held this seat for over 50 years, but they have done nothing for us. This is not true of Modiji, we will give him our vote.' Not wanting to be left out, his neighbour, a barber, chimed in, 'This time, I will give my vote to Modiji since he has brought us the temple after 500 years. If not him, who? Sonia Gandhi? She sits in Delhi, not here, she doesn't work here. She has come here with great difficulty perhaps three times, but no development has happened. Look at Banaras and Ayodhya, everywhere there is work happening but not here.'

This was to be a familiar sentiment that echoed across the city as we drove down a road full of potholes and flanked by nullahs on both sides. The air was thick with dust, new infrastructure had clearly not reached here. We stopped to have a chat with Tripathiji who was reading a newspaper. I asked him to share his views about the state of the INDIA bloc and his thoughts on the statement made by Bhagwant Mann on the intention of the Aam Aadmi Party (AAP) to contest from all seats in Punjab and Mamata Banerjee refusing an alliance with the Congress in West Bengal.

This is what he had to say, 'Bhaiya, *yeh sab kursi ka khel hain*, everyone wants the chair. They are all *chor*, and all are coming now to save their seats. It was always going to crumble (the alliance). In 2024, Modiji will come, look at how much work he is doing along with the mandir.'

Just further down, some people were huddled by a fire in the bitter cold. I asked them about how the Congress has developed the city. One of the men replied, 'They have held it since Independence and no work has been done. We had no alternative but to vote for them then, but we do now, and we will vote for Modiji.'

Afterwards, having spoken to women and some youth, it became amply clear to me that in the heart of the Congress stronghold, there was a strong pro-Narendra Modi sentiment. More than 60 per cent of women and 65 per cent of the youth there wanted Narendra Modi to return as our prime minister.

I was shocked to see this level of anti-incumbency in Raebareli, a seat held by Sonia Gandhi for decades. Before her, Prime Minister Indira Gandhi had won from Raebareli thrice. The constituency also elected Feroze Gandhi twice in 1952 and 1957. The party has secured more than 50 per cent of the votes eight times, including all four elections fought by Sonia Gandhi. The party has held on to this, the Congress bastion, in all but three Lok Sabha elections since 1951; however, its vote share has been decreasing with each election by 7–10 percentage points. In 2009, it won the seat with 72.23 per cent of the vote share; this dropped to 62.83 per cent in 2014 and by 2019 it was at 55.80 per cent. The Congress's worst performance was in 1996 and 1998 when it got less than 10 per cent of the votes. Is the Congress heading that way? Perhaps this is why Sonia Gandhi will not contest from here this year. The Jan Ki Baat data analysis tells me that Raebareli can be won by the BJP in 2024 if it fields a strong candidate and that the margin will be big.

It is clear that 2024 will go the prime minister's way because '*ab sub kuch Ayodhya hain*'.

2

Super NDA

vs

INDIA Bloc

'Politics may make strange bedfellows, but historical opponents rarely become friends, and end up losing their base vote in overestimating arithmetic over chemistry in politics.'

The boatmen of Varanasi are a politically savvy group. They ferry pilgrims and tourists who spill the world into their boats. I was making a beeline for the city to get a feel of the political buzz for the 2024 Lok Sabha Elections albeit at a snail's pace for there were intense foggy conditions—not in the mind of the Indian voters though. We drove at a slow speed because the visibility was not even there for two metres. Suddenly, my reporter Chandan Pandey and analyst Sandeep swivelled around to look at me. Pandey exclaimed breathlessly, 'Sir, look at what has happened!'

Startled, I enquired, 'What has happened, Pandey? '*Sub kuch ghar mein theek hain* (Is all well at home?)?'

He answered, 'Yes, yes, all is well at home. Look what has happened in the political circles. It is being reported that Nitish Kumar is holding talks with the BJP for a tie-up.'

What was new in that? Nitish was known for changing camps and alliances at the drop of a hat. He always sways in the direction in which the wind is blowing. But this was a clear unravelling of the newly stitched together alliance INDIA.

Who Is the Real Enemy of the Indian National Developmental Inclusive Alliance?

When the Indian National Developmental Inclusive Alliance (INDIA) bloc was stitched on 18 July 2023, I tweeted that it was nothing but a political joke. Unfortunately, the joke is at the expense of the populace. The Opposition parties are banking on the INDIA bloc to overthrow Prime Minister Modi in the 2024 General Elections. Post alliance, the Trinamool Congress (TMC) leader Derek O'Brien tweeted that it was a 'Fantastic PR campaign'. Since the day it was roped together, I have always maintained that this so-called alliance is a farce because *there is no alliance.*

Why? Well, look at the manner it was brought about.

Political alliances are a product of the organic ability of vote transferability between parties and a shared political interest. They do not happen by leaders merely sitting together and conducting an all-party meeting. This alliance's only agenda is to overthrow the Modi government, *they have absolutely nothing else in common.*

It behoves us to dissect this strange and inherently contradictory amalgamation called INDIA. What is it all about? Is it, perchance, a rebranded version of the UPA? The *mahagathbandhan* (grand coalition) as a new version of the UPA, destined to crush the BJP? I could to an extent agree with the prematurely enthusiastic O'Brien— Mamata Banerjee was spitting fire at Rahul Gandhi and the Congress at the time of writing this chapter and by the time I finished the book she had left the alliance. *This is a fantastic PR campaign?*

As the election draws closer and the political climate gets more volatile, I would have to say that it is a perfect example of how to score a self-goal. The crux of any political alliance is a meeting of minds through which strategies can successfully lead to transfer of votes. The leaders act as catalyst to enable their workers at the grassroots to join hands with workers from other parties. This is anything but that. Let me elaborate this by the following example.

2019 Mahagathbandhan: A Deep Dive

I recall that in the run-up to the 2019 General Elections, I was in UP traversing across constituencies when I got a call from a journalist who gleefully proclaimed that the BJP now has no chance in the upcoming election. I was surprised by this deduction and enquired about the logic behind his conclusion.

He stated, 'Well, now Mayawati and Akhilesh have joined forces.'

The Samajwadi Party (SP) and the Bahujan Samaj Party (BSP) had announced the Mahagathbandhan, an anti-BJP, anti-Congress alliance.

I said that this would mean that the BJP vote share would increase. He mocked my suggestion and called me an idiot.

Taken aback at his rude tone, I clarified that the transfer of votes between the two will not occur.

He curtly replied, 'You understand nothing.'

And cut me off.

When the verdict came, the BJP's vote share in UP increased from 41.57 per cent in 2017 to 49.60 per cent in 2019, an increase of 8.03 per cent points! The SP vote share dipped by more than around 4 per cent. Of course, that same journalist did not take my calls after the Mahagathbandhan proved to be a failure. The logic behind my prediction was clear. I was speaking to people and retrieving data from the ground, and the information was that neither the workers of the BSP nor the SP were happy with the alliance. And there was a good reason for this.

Historically, the Samajwadi Party has always believed that the Bahujan Samaj Party stood in opposition to them. The core vote base of the SP was mainly the Yadavs, and the BSP's core voter was predominantly the Scheduled Castes (SC). Whenever the BSP got the Brahmin votes, it was an unbeatable combination. In addition, the BSP attracted the non-Yadav OBC vote as well, apart from the Muslim vote, and hence could win elections. In this sense, both parties saw themselves as political rivals. Over the past 10–15 years, especially, in UP politics, these two parties were each other's rather volatile political enemies. Who can forget the infamous guesthouse episode when Mulayam Singh Yadav was at the helm of affairs?

Hence, when BSP supremo Mayawati and SP president Akhilesh Yadav held a joint press conference in 2019 to announce the Mahagathbandhan, it was clear that it was an alliance of the leaders, not an alliance of the workers on the ground. My findings from the polls and surveys indicated that the core Jatav SC votes, hitherto loyal to Mayawati, and the core Bahujan vote of the BSP were not voting in favour of the SP, nor were the loyal Yadav voters of the SP drifting to the BSP. This was unbelievable to many until the results were declared. The SP saw a dip of their vote share by 4 per cent over 2014 and the Jatav SC votes of Mayawati drifted to the BJP on seats from where the SP candidates were contesting.

Thus, I knew that if these two come together, their voters would transfer to the BJP instead, and this is exactly what happened. The BSP still managed to get a few seats from some of its core areas, but the SP could gain no advantage and was the bigger loser. In fact, I had written in the *Financial Express* in June 2019 that this 'new trend—the division of Jatav SC votes, and their movement towards the BJP—began to emerge in 2014 and has consolidated further in 2019'.

In 2019, the increase of the BJP vote share to 49 per cent in UP meant that an alliance that looked very strong on paper arithmetically ended up in a situation where both the parties lost, establishing my thesis that alliances do not just happen arithmetically. *For the arithmetic to work, chemistry must happen.* And the social base that the BSP and the SP represent individually cannot be merged with each other.

Similarly, in the run-up to the 2024 elections, the parties of the INDIA bloc are handicapped by the fact that neither their workers nor their voters are complementary to each other; if anything, they are antithetical to each other. The leaders can hold as many meetings as they want, at the end of the day it is a matter of political survival for the workers on the ground. The competition is fierce; hence, there is no sense in supporting such an alliance because the worker and the local candidate know that if an alliance member wins from their constituency, this will end up jeopardizing the political career of the worker. So, instead of Narendra Modi or the BJP, the bigger enemy is the worker of individual parties that form the INDIA bloc.

Why Is the INDIA Bloc Crumbling?

The INDIA bloc parties are inherently averse to each other. There is no glue that can hold them together.

AAP vs Congress Rivalry

Let us look at the combination of the Congress and AAP. The growth of the AAP happened at the cost of the Congress and not at the cost of the BJP. The Congress had a stranglehold in Punjab, yet it was the AAP that swept the 2019 elections. In January 2024, Chief Minister Bhagwant Mann stated that the AAP will win all 13 Lok Sabha seats in Punjab hinting that there is hardly any chance of AAP's alliance with the Congress in Punjab despite being part of the INDIA bloc.

In Gujarat, the debutant AAP increased its vote share from 0.6 per cent in 2017 to almost 13 per cent in 2022 and finished second in at least 30 assembly constituencies in Gujarat. It bled the Congress and not the BJP, contrary to popular perception that the AAP's presence in the bipolar polity of the state would dent both the Congress and the BJP votes.

In Delhi, the AAP has forged ahead, reducing the vote share of the Congress to a single digit. The Congress has been relegated to a third position in the UT. Hence the AAP and the Congress coming together in Delhi will not cut into BJP vote shares for the 2024 General Elections either. The BJP will sweep Delhi this year. I am confident about this because when travelling around Delhi, particularly post the consecration of the Ram Mandir, every second person said that they are bringing back Prime Minister Modi to power in the upcoming Lok Sabha elections—the Assembly elections are a different matter though.

TMC vs the Left Power Tussle

The INDIA bloc has completely unravelled in Bengal where the CPI(M)-led Left has been up in arms against the TMC. The TMC and the Left parties in Bengal have never had their workers uniting at the grassroots level, and none had a shared political agenda. In fact, Bengal's Chief Minister Mamata Banerjee's politics germinates on the anti-Left plank. She was beaten with lathis when the Left was ruling the state. An astute politician, Didi knows that if she lets the Left get even a small foothold, her long-term political existence will be threatened. And the Left considers Mamata as their political nemesis.

TMC vs Congress Fight

The TMC and the Congress partnership is a farce with contradicting situations arising at regular intervals. The equation between the state Congress unit and the TMC has also been tense and acrimonious, with the relations between Mamata and West Bengal Pradesh Congress Committee (WBPCC) president Adhir Ranjan Chowdhury marred by hostility and bitterness for many years. She was very clear from the beginning that if there was to be an alliance with Congress, she could not give them more than two seats, yet the Congress insisted on six seats. If the Congress fought only two seats, Adhir's future will be threatened. Despite being an alliance partner, Adhir was not reined in and continued to take potshots at the TMC supremo. In no uncertain terms, the TMC expressed frustration with the seat-sharing talks. Mamata also expressed her displeasure that the Congress had not informed her that its ongoing Bharat Jodo Nyay Yatra would enter West Bengal. 'Even as a matter of courtesy they didn't tell that they are coming to my state. I am part of INDIA alliance (*The Hindu*, 24 January 2024).'

Mamata dumped the alliance on 24 January 2024, two days after the inauguration of the Ram Mandir in Ayodhya.

The collapse of relations between the TMC and the Congress was a forgone conclusion. Mamata's decision was not a knee-jerk reaction to the failed seat-sharing agreement with the Congress, it was about securing her party's future in Bengal. She knows she is the only force that can take on the BJP in her state. The Congress is irrelevant. She also knows that even if the BJP comes to power in Bengal, she can still mark her time in the Opposition but if the Left or the Congress rise in the state, they will take away a core vote which is the Muslim vote, and that can spell the end for her party. After all, in the past, many of the Left party members had jumped ship when she formed the TMC, so the CPI (M)-led Left and Congress are a larger threat to Mamata. Moreover, the TMC cannot afford to ally with the Left parties because of the negative ramifications in the next Assembly elections; the public does not forget opportunism.

Nitish's Declining Popularity

Let us go back to Bihar Chief Minister Nitish Kumar. His split from the INDIA bloc is not news to me because

Nitish's antics are beyond déjà vu! What beats me is how the INDIA bloc presumed Bihar was theirs for the taking with him as an ally when the only consistent factor is that Nitish changes his political alliances at every given opportune moment. He has a history of changing alliances and there is nothing that can be done to change that. With the alliance openly stating that the prana pratishtha at the Ram Mandir is of no political importance, Nitish's position in Bihar weakened further. This is a major fault line in the alliance.

During my reconnaissance in Ayodhya, I met Ravi from Gopalganj, Bihar. He was part of a large group. When I got to know that he hailed from Bihar, I asked, 'So, you've come from Lalu's home?'

He replied. 'It might be Lalu's home but now everything is about Bhagwan Ram. *Joh Ram ko layein hain, hum unko layenge.*'

The rest of the group heartily agreed.

Bad miscalculation on behalf of the alliance. With this, I knew I was getting the sentiment from the ground in Bihar. We will see Prime Minister Modi voted back to power in large numbers like in 2014 and 2019. Any good reader of politics in Bihar can judge that Nitish's political credibility is at its lowest. The Janata Dal (United) [JD(U)] is an ever-shrinking party. Over the last three elections, the party's seat share has been reducing. In fact, when the JD(U) fought alone in 2014, it could not breach the 20 per cent mark. In 2019, when it fought along with the BJP, it could cross the 20 per cent vote share mark. But the last time when Nitish jumped ship to be with the Rashtriya Janata Dal (RJD) he had miffed the BJP heavily. So, the BJP was very clear that even if Nitish is taken back, it will not be on his terms. Nitish found himself in a political situation where he had never been before. If he continued to be with the RJD, after the Lok Sabha elections, Lalu would demand his son be made the chief minister. If he went to the BJP, he would have to agree to the BJP's terms. In either scenario, it was very clear that Nitish did not have the upper hand at the negotiating table. He had only and only joined the INDIA bloc with the hope that he would be made the prime ministerial candidate. Much to his chagrin Mamata and Arvind Kejriwal proposed Mallikarjun Kharge's name as the prime ministerial candidate. That was the last nail in the coffin. Nitish's hopes were dashed and there was no reason for him to remain with this alliance.

Prime Minister Modi's political acumen can be gauged when he announced the Bharat Ratna for former two-time chief minister of Bihar Karpoori Thakurji, who has been an icon and a flagbearer of social justice. He worked for upliftment of the backward castes as well as the economically weaker sections in the forward castes. Soon after Prime Minister Modi made the announcement, the JD (U) supremo took a swipe at dynastic politics. To quote an *Indian Express* article (25 January 2024), Nitish said, 'Karpoori never promoted his family ... [L]ike Karpoori, I have not promoted my family in politics.' This was obviously a dig at Lalu Prasad Yadav because Nitish knows that with this announcement even the slightest chance of the backward castes coming together with the INDIA bloc was gone.

The bottom line is that the JD(U) is not the future of Bihar. And I will not be surprised if in the next few years, the party gets dissolved and many of its members switch to the RJD or the BJP. There are 40 Lok Sabha constituencies in Bihar. The alliance was built with the presumption that they will sweep Bihar, but they simply could not keep it together in the state.

The Rise of the Super NDA

Apart from Bihar, another state where the alliance was banking on heavily was Maharashtra. But here too there were enough political signals to conclude that the alliance was over. With the NCP split into two, Sharad Pawar has become inconsistent in his criticism of the ruling establishment. The BJP contested from 24 seats in the 2014 General Elections and 25 in 2019, winning 23 seats both times.

Now with Eknath Shinde and Ajit Pawar joining the NDA, the alliance has become stronger in Maharashtra than what it was in the run-up to 2019 because out of the 15 per cent vote that Sharad Pawar's NCP used to have, a large chunk moved with Ajit Pawar. Similarly, Uddhav Thackeray got 20 per cent of the votes in 2019 because of the transferability from the National Democratic Alliance (NDA) and Prime Minister Modi. Thackeray got votes on the BJP name, not his name in the Lok Sabha elections. With Shinde coming into the BJP fold, and success of the NDA's seat-sharing ability, the BJP intends to fight more than 25 seats, possibly bettering its wins in Maharashtra than in 2014 and 2019. Thus, the Maharashtra NDA is a super NDA.

Sharad Pawar understands the pulse of Maharashtra like none other. He knows that the wave in the state is in favour of Prime Minister Modi and hence instead of being a harsh critic of the BJP and Prime Minister Modi, he has toned down his criticism. The baseline of Maharashtra politics has changed with Thackeray being the biggest loser and the NDA poised to gain massively in the run-up to 2024. In fact, even as I write this chapter there seems to be an exodus towards the Super NDA in Maharashtra.

The Congress's Short-sightedness

The INDIA bloc's pathetic plight continues. After Arvind and Mamata proposed Kharge as the prime ministerial candidate of the alliance, Kharge's response was telling. He said, 'Let's win first, then we will see (*The Economic Times*, 20 December 2023).'

The alliance partners of the Congress are not confident about defeating Prime Minister Modi. They know that Rahul Gandhi is a reluctant heir, a political lightweight, and cannot be taken seriously, but still came together in an alliance! This alliance is only trying to slow down the Modi juggernaut and trying to limit the BJP to less than 272 seats in the Lok Sabha. They are aware that the Ram Mandir is going to carry away the elections, and since they cannot defeat Prime Minister Modi, they are aiming to keep the BJP numbers down. In my opinion, it is not possible for them to defeat Modi or even restrict him. If they had a smarter political adviser, they would have attended the prana pratishtha of Ram Lalla at the Ram Mandir. It would have been a politically savvy thing to do. But the Congress's fear of losing the Muslim vote made them take a bad political decision, which they will live to regret for years to come. Many view this move of theirs as a slight against the Hindus; as lack of interest in them as a community. Another nail in the coffin of the alliance.

INDIA Bloc Members Disrespect of Hinduism

Then there are these rather unfortunate comments about Hinduism and Sanatan Dharma from the DMK leaders in Tamil Nadu like DMK MP A. Raja's ('Indians living in other countries also propagating castes in the name of Hindu religion, so Hindu religion is the biggest menace not only to India, now it becomes menace to the entire world', *The Hindustan Times*, 14 March 2024) and Udhayanidhi Stalin's insults against the Sanatan Dharma have left a bad taste in the mouth of the Hindu voter. A majority of the Hindus found these remarks repulsive. The DMK leaders said this to please their constituencies; thus the state took precedence over the nation. Since the DMK is an active member of the INDIA bloc, such statements will have grave repercussions.

I was among tribals in Jharkhand when Udhayanidhi made the infamous statement: 'Just like dengue, mosquitoes, malaria, or coronavirus need to be eradicated, we have to eradicate Sanatana (*The Hindu*, 3 September 2023).'

Guess what?

A tribal had seen a video of his speech on WhatsApp and said, 'These people are making a big mistake, we will never vote for them.'

How can these players not see the possible fallout of such politics? Such a political stance will make it extremely difficult to do politics in major parts of India. Hence, it is hard to take this alliance seriously and that is why I call it a farce.

Confusion and Chaos at the Grassroots Level

As mentioned earlier, the crux of the matter is that even the workers within each party are unhappy with this alliance because they know that it affects their political survival. Imagine that somebody has been preparing to fight in the Lok Sabha from constituency X. And suddenly the alliance takes place and the rival against whom he has been preparing to contest against all this while gets the ticket instead. It is but natural that the contestant of either party from that constituency will not work for the alliance partner. For example, if the Congress and the AAP come together in Delhi, the Congress worker will not work for the AAP and vice versa because the workers know deep down that Prime Minister Modi is coming back in 2024 and if one of them becomes stronger, the political survival of the other becomes an issue.

To cut a long story short, if we look for a winning alliance this is not the one. Beats me why sections of the polity and the media were calling it a *strong* alliance? It seems that they have forgotten the previous chest thumping in the run-up to the 2019 elections. Remember what Mamata said at an Eid gathering in Bengal in 2019? She said, '*Jo humse takrayega, woh choor choor ho jayega* (anyone who takes us on will be demolished), *Indian Express*, 5 June 2019.'

Prime Minister Modi had said that the BJP would garner 300+ Lok Sabha seats, which they did, and their vote share also increased to over 37 per cent. It is looking like the same situation is going to recur in the 2024 General Elections. Hence, I maintain that this INDIA bloc is nothing but a big political joke.

Politics may make strange bedfellows, but historical opponents rarely become friends, and end up losing their base vote in overestimating arithmetic over chemistry in politics.

Rahul Gandhi's Poor Leadership

The unravelling of the INDIA bloc is also because of the absence of a credible leader, and a party that could act

Prime Minister Narendra Modi at a rally in Palnadu, Andhra Pradesh on 17 March 2024. Photo courtesy: Narendra Modi's X account.

Prime Minister Narendra Modi attends a Nari Shakti Vandan Abhinandan programme in Barasat, West Bengal on 6 March 2024.
Photo courtesy: Narendra Modi website on YouTube.
These two have been the most defining in political rallies in March 2024. An increase in the NDA tally in both states will increase its probability to either be near or cross 400 seats.

At Shri Ram Mandir, Ayodhya, 22 January 2024. Yes, I was there.

With the youth of Bihar who are determined to take it forward

Speaking to the Matua community in Krishnanagar, Bengal. Their happiness after the notification of Citizenship Amendment Act (CAA, 2019) was reflective in our conversation.

Always on the move. I have always followed one principle, be among the people to experience Bharat. 400 Lok Sabha constituencies, one lakh km, 40 Indian elections and counting...

Shooting on the streets of Puri, Odisha. It is a swing seat in Odisha.

Arriving in my home town Indore to a rousing welcome

Stopping at a hotel to have poha and jalebi on the way to Neemuch, Madhya Pradesh

Speaking to voters along the roadside in Old Bengaluru. Political wisdom of the comman man is often underrated and undervalued by traditional analysts.

In Dharavi, Mumbai, understanding if political narrative of Opposition parties have any takers

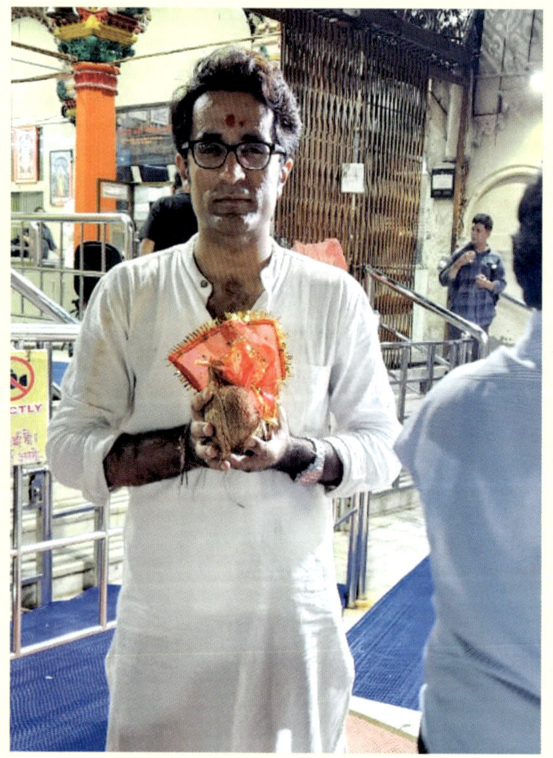

*Bhakti mein shakti hai.
At Mumba Devi Mandir,
Mumbai.*

Speaking to rural voters on the way to Adilabad, Telangana. At the core of every voter's expectations are needs and aspirations that need to met.

Blessed to have a hot meal at Annapurna on the way to Nilgiris from Coimbatore, Tamil Nadu

Speaking to women voters in Coimbatore, Tamil Nadu

At Puliakulam Vinayagar Temple, Coimbatore, the one which terrorists wanted to blow up in 2022

as an anchor of the Opposition unity. Rahul Gandhi's credibility is at its lowest, and hence the Congress is not getting stronger electorally. The members of the bloc do not trust his political maturity and are of the belief that his inexperience will end up jeopardizing their own political fortunes. Remember that photo taken on 18 July 2023 of varied party leaders of the INDIA bloc with Rahul? Most of them have left.

The alliance partners were desperately hoping that the Congress could defeat the BJP in the Assembly elections held in December 2023, and that would act as a catalyst for it in the run- up to the 2024 Lok Sabha Elections. However, the BJP's sweep in the Assembly elections in three states made it clear to all major alliance partners—the Congress is only good at losing elections.

When I was in Raebareli conducting surveys and polls for the upcoming general elections, I found the Congress receding in its bastion. In 2009, the Congress garnered a vote of more than 70 per cent, which has dipped by around 7–10 per cent over the last two Lok Sabha elections. Under such circumstances, the alliance's chances are slim. Over the past many months, despite multiple meetings of the leaders, the INDIA bloc could not hold a single joint press conference or declare a consensus candidate or release a common minimum programme.

Since the BJP came to power at the Centre in 2014, the Congress has been spiralling downwards. It has lost crucial states such as UP and Maharashtra and even backyard constituencies that the party has held over decades. Table 1 reflects the contest between the two parties.

Table 1: BJP and Congress Vote Share (1952–2019)

Election Year	Largest Party	Seats Won	Vote Share	2nd Largest Party	Seat Won	Vote Share
2019	BJP	303	37.36%	INC	52	19.49%
2014	BJP	282	31.00%	INC	44	19.31%
2009	INC	206	28.55%	BJP	116	18.80%
2004	INC	145	26.53%	BJP	138	22.16%
1999	BJP	182	23.75%	INC	114	28.30%
1998	BJP	182	25.59%	INC	141	25.82%
1996	BJP	161	20.29%	INC (I)	140	28.80%
1991	INC (I)	244	36.40%	BJP	120	20.07%
1989	INC (I)	197	39.53%	JD	143	17.79%
1984	INC (I)	414	46.86%	TDP	30	4.31%
1980	INC (I)	353	42.69%	JP (S)	41	9.39%
1977	JP	209	41.32%	INC (R)	198	34.52%
1971	INC (R)	352	43.68%	CPI (M)	25	5.12%
1967	INC	283	40.78%	ABJS	35	9.31%
1962	INC	361	44.72%	CPI	29	9.94%
1957	INC	371	47.78%	CPI	27	8.92%
1952	INC	364	44.99%	CPI	16	3.29%

Source: Jan Ki Baat data analysis

Prime Minister Modi Establishing a Psychological Advantage

With the Congress poised to lose Raebareli, there is a strong possibility that their total number of seats in the Lok Sabha may drop below 40. In a blistering speech made in February this year, Prime Minister Modi said, 'I pray that you are able to secure 40 seats (*India Today*, 7 February 2024).'

He even called the party outdated.

He added that he could, 'gauge the mood of the nation', and that the country 'will definitely give the NDA more than 400 seats and the BJP at least 370 seats (*The Hindu*, 5 February 2024).'

The Congress has not just lost elections at the Lok Sabha and Assembly levels, more worryingly, it has seen a steady drain of its members.

Now in politics, it is a fact that you set targets that are clear. Psephologically, when the sentiment on the ground is largely in favour of a particular party coming to power, voters sitting on the fence will vote for that party. This is why gaining a positive political momentum is extremely important in an election. The BJP in 2024 has such a momentum and there is a unanimous sentiment across various sections of society across India that Prime Minister Modi is returning for a third term. Voters who have till now been in two minds could end up voting for the BJP and hence increase its winning margins.

NDA Increasing by Strength

The INDIA bloc came into being in July 2023 but within eight months, it has only become weaker while the NDA is rapidly gaining ground. There are critics who say members of the NDA are not important to the BJP.

If the members of the NDA are irrelevant, why do more and more parties want to join it?

There are talks that a super NDA might emerge from Andhra Pradesh. The BJP has the support of 37 regional parties at the time of writing this chapter, with the possibility of more tying up with the NDA. Thus, the BJP under the leadership of Narendra Modi is an ever-expanding political unit and the INDIA bloc is an ever-shrinking one. In 2024, vis-à-vis 2019, there are 11 states where the BJP has a chance to increase its presence and 9 states where it can continue to hold on to the seats it won in the last general elections. I will discuss this in details later in the book.

The Alliance's Inability to Set a Narrative for 2024

The INDIA bloc lacks not only political cohesion, but also a common agenda. Supriya Shrinate, national spokesperson of the Congress, describes Rahul Gandhi as 'Jan Nayak', a conscience keeper of the nation. Unfortunately, the need of the hour is one of political astuteness, something that the voters find grossly missing in Rahul.

The Congress has been at the helm of political power for more than 50 years and that may have led to complacency. In modern times, to run a political party, you need workers on the ground to act as a well-oiled machine, carrying forward the party's manifesto to every voter. Elections are won by successfully changing electoral mood in your party's favour, not by running a campaign against your opponents. The campaign against Narendra Modi flopped in 2019, yet Rahul continues with Modi bashing. The name-calling by Rahul is an indication of the deep-seated sense of entitlement in our political system. There is a strong belief in a section of the political establishment that only one family has the right to rule over the country.

The result of this stubborn ineptitude could end up creating a situation where the Congress performs poorer than 2019 in the forthcoming Lok Sabha elections. This is the reason the political parties of the alliance have started distancing themselves from the Congress.

INDIA Bloc's Lack of Political Acumen

Now let us take a deep dive into the NDA strategy. The BJP and the NDA are moving forward methodically. On the occasion of the National Voters' Day, just two days after the prana pratishtha ceremony at the Ram Mandir, Prime Minister Modi interacted with lakhs of first-time voters from more than 5,000 locations virtually and urged them to defeat family-run parties with the strength of their votes. He asserted that the youth has always been his priority. He reiterated the immense potential they held in steering the country towards progress and development. He asked them to share their aspirations for the Bharat of 2047.

The prime minister has instructed the BJP to increase its lead margins in the booths which it had led in 2019. At the same time, the party has identified seats where they lost, and by what margins in the 2019 General Elections. He is not resting on his laurels. The BJP is expanding in the areas where it is strong and strengthening the areas where it is weak. The party is focusing on regions that they have not yet got a foothold. The BJP led by the prime minister is an ever-expanding unit.

If you compare the political harmony of the INDIA bloc to the NDA, the former is locked in a cycle of pulling each other down. They stomped on Nitish and other parties who had thought to use the caste census as a politically galvanizing tool of 2024. This was also one of the reasons Nitish shifted to the NDA.

On the other hand, the NDA is using all political tools to move forward. Recently, the Modi government conferred the Bharat Ratna to politicians from across the political spectrum: former Prime Minister P.V. Narasimha Rao (Congress), former Prime Minister Chaudhary Charan Singh (Janata Party), former Deputy Prime Minister L.K. Advani (BJP) and former Chief Minister of Bihar Karpoori Thakur (Janata Party, Secular). Then, of course, the INDIA bloc has misread the mood of the nation by boycotting the prana pratishtha of Shri Ram at the Ram Mandir.

There is a big difference between the leadership quality of Rahul Gandhi and Narendra Modi.

Prime Minister Modi converts every challenge into an opportunity because he has over 10 years of experience at the grassroots level, more than 15 years of experience in the *sangathan* and over 22 years of experience in governance. Narendra Modi is a once-in-a-generation leader.

Rahul Gandhi on the other hand is a failed product despite many launches. He is the scion of a powerful political family but is a reluctant politician with no political acumen so to speak, which explains the Congress's shrinking presence pan India.

This is why the INDIA bloc tried to peddle a north vs south narrative, which too did not gain any steam. The BJP is *not* a political untouchable in the southern states.

Getting the North–South Narrative Wrong

In three out of five southern states, the BJP has a strong and formidable presence.

Tamil Nadu

In Tamil Nadu, the BJP's vote share increased in 2019 and in 2024 it should increase again.

The party is expanding its social base with a strong leader like K. Annamalai on the ground even in Tamil Nadu, which was considered to be politically allergic to the BJP type of politics. My reporters have analysed that in parts of southern Tamil Nadu, the anti-BJP sentiment does not exist—Prime Minister Modi is accepted. This is reflected in the prime minister's Kashi Tamil Sangamam, a political masterstroke that attacks at the root of anti-Centre politics purported by the DMK.

The Kashi Tamil Sangamam seeks to celebrate north and south India's historical and civilizational connections. When the prime minister inaugurated it in Varanasi in 2023, he had the following observation to make, 'Kashi Tamil Sangamam furthers the spirit of "Ek Bharat, Shrestha Bharat" (Press Information Bureau, 17 December 2023).' He recalled the establishment of the sacred Sengol in the new Parliament under the supervision of the Aadinam saints reflecting the same spirit of Ek Bharat, Shrestha Bharat. 'This flow of spirit of "Ek Bharat, Shrestha Bharat" is infusing the soul of our nation today.' He further emphasized the need for knowing each other's culture as this increases trust and develops rapport.

You will recall that I met many pilgrims from the Tamil Sangamam at the Ram Mandir. One of them was Mridula from Chennai, who had come with her children. When I asked her how it feels to have Shri Ram's darshan, she said, 'heavenly', and started to smile and cry at the same time. She added, 'My mother and grandmother used to recite stories of

Prabhu Shri Ram to me when I was a kid. It is marvellous that I got this darshan… got see Prabhu Shri Ram's Mandir in my lifetime. But I am sad that my mother and grandmother passed away without being able to do so.'

These are the emotions of the people from Tamil Nadu.

It remains to be seen how many seats the BJP will win from here, but there will definitely be an increment in its vote share, and we may also see a surprising seat share in the state. Therefore, even in Tamil Nadu the BJP is stronger than it was in 2019.

Karnataka

In Karnataka, the BJP in alliance with the Janata Dal-Secular [JD(S)] is a formidable force. The JD(S) headed by former Prime Minister H.D. Deve Gowda has historically been a significant third player in Karnataka, where the Congress and the BJP have been the two main parties. The BJP, as the leader of the NDA, believes that forming an alliance with the JD(S) will enhance its prospects in the 2024 Lok Sabha polls, particularly in south Karnataka.

Andhra Pradesh

In Andhra Pradesh, the BJP has allied with Chandrababu Naidu's Telugu Desam Party (TDP) and Pawan Kalyan's

Jan Sena Party for the upcoming Lok Sabha and Andhra Pradesh Assembly elections respectively, which will be held simultaneously. Therefore, the BJP in the southern states is stronger than the Congress, not weaker. For the Congress, the lazy political experiment INDIA has fallen faster than a pack of cards.

Telangana

In Telangana, the BJP's base is stronger than what it was in 2019. Despite losing the Assembly elections in December 2023, the party has doubled its vote share and won eight seats over only a single one in the 2018 elections. Of the eight seats the BJP won, seven came from north Telangana. The winners are also either first-timers or newcomers into the party. Most strikingly, BJP's K. Venkata Ramana Reddy defeated Bharat Rashtra Samithi (BRS) supremo K. Chandrashekar Rao.

Prime Minister Modi's Stellar Performance

The Jan Ki Baat poll survey indicates that even the Congress vote will transfer to the BJP because of the Modi wave in 2024.

In 2014, lesser people knew Narendra Modi, yet he won with an absolute majority. Some could say, there was an anti-incumbency. Five years later, more people knew of the prime minister and hence the BJP could roundly defeat the anti-incumbency factor and won with an even larger mandate. In 2024, people are in ananda, and hence the sentiment is strongly in favour of Prime Minister Modi, and I will not be surprised if the NDA surpasses its performance in 2019.

Prime Minister Modi is in the hearts and the minds of the aam janta. Many consider him to be the builder of modern India or modern civilizational Bharat. People say he has done what no prime minister could ever do. He has got the Ram Mandir built in Ayodhya; he has got Article 370 removed; he has brought peace in the Jammu Kashmir Valley. Many believe that he runs a zero corruption, zero leakages government. His foreign policy initiatives are being appreciated by the populace.

I asked my taxi driver Montu in Bengal about his opinion on the political agenda of the INDIA bloc, 'Why do they (Opposition) vehemently oppose Modi when he is clearly working for the betterment of the people? He has built the Ram Mandir, he has raised the maan-samman of the nation, so why should they oppose …'

He interrupted me by showing me a video and said, 'Here is French President Macron. Modiji is doing a roadshow with him in Jaipur. We have never seen anything like this in our lives.'

Prime Minister Modi is seen as a member of the family and somebody who will always keep India's interests supreme. In fact, he has become a civilizational icon. I think that after Mahatma Gandhi, Narendra Modi is the only leader to enjoy such respect among the masses.

The difference between the NDA and the INDIA bloc reflects the difference between Varanasi and Raebareli models of development. The Raebareli model represents the INDIA bloc model of development, and the Varanasi model represents Prime Minister Modi's model of development.

If you travel today to Varanasi, you will find 90 per cent of the people praising the prime minister because the city has been completely transformed both economically and spiritually under his leadership. There is great joy in the hearts and minds of the people. There is immense *garv* in being a Banarasi. The ghats have been cleaned and tourism is at an all-time high, leading to an economic upliftment of those living in the city.

Prime Minister Modi has laid the foundation stone of a world-class cricket stadium—Varanasi is only growing. The stadium will be developed at a cost of about ₹450 crore and spread across an area of more than 30 acres (PM India website, 23 September 2023). This has happened just in a matter of nine years ever since the prime minister won the constituency in 2014. Prime Minister Modi's development has brought Varanasi on the global map in a new form.

Compare this to what the Gandhi family has done for Raebareli over the past 30–40 years. It is in a poorly developed state with many roads either dug up or riddled with potholes. You will not find a proper internet connection in a majority of the houses there, and the street corners look dirty. The residents of the city will tell you that Sonia Gandhi hardly visits them.

Again, this is in stark contrast to the regular visits of Prime Minister Modi to Varanasi. Narendra Modi's politics is about developmental surplus, civilizational renaissance, taking pride in one's cultural identity and improving the country's image on the global map.

On the other hand, the Gandhi family's politics is *rajshahi*, which is about depriving development, consolidating the minority vote, dividing the majority vote and thinking that they deserve to rule the nation forever. It is this mentality that has made the party ignore the red flags in the past few years. The party's vote share has been continuously dwindling from 72 per cent in 2009 to 55 per cent in 2019 (The *Indian Express*, 16 February 2024) and it is on the verge of losing the constituency. No effort has been undertaken by the Congress high command to make any course correction.

Rahul too has the same approach towards his constituency Amethi, which he has represented several times since 2002. When he realized that the popular sentiment was not in his favour, instead of improving the conditions of his constituency, he fled to Wayanad for an easy win. The late Arun Jaitley was absolutely correct when he said that Rahul is responsible for reducing the grand old party into a fringe 'two-digit' party (*The Economic Times*, 8 May 2018).

To conclude, the INDIA bloc's breakdown has become apparent, while the NDA has only grown stronger with time. I will not be surprised if Prime Minister Modi, riding on the surging popularity because of his excellent implementation of policies, surpasses his tally in 2019 in both vote share and seat share. In 2014, he won 90 per cent of the seats from across 60 per cent of India; in 2019 that social and geographical base increased further. Now in the run-up to the 2024 General Elections, his social base and connection with the people of India is much more than in 2019 and the Opposition is weaker than what it was then. It seems that it is not the BJP who is fighting this election alone; after 22 January, Prime Minister Modi has made 2024 a 'people's election'.

3

The 2024 General Elections

A Psephological Analysis

'Narendra Modi 3.0 will be stronger and bigger. Only a political black swan event can change this.'

I think I was born to analyse the elections of this great country. Conducting surveys gives me an enviable opportunity to travel the length and breadth of Bharat and meet its citizens. The objective of the Jan Ki Baat team is to reflect the public view about the candidates, parties and specific issues at the time the poll is conducted. In this chapter, I have presented the findings of the opinion polls conducted from January to February 2024 for the 18th Lok Sabha Elections.

Jan Ki Baat Probability Map of Outcome Model

The Jan Ki Baat Probability Map of Outcome Model has performed random sampling across each state of India to give a constituency-wise and district-wise analysis. The sample size was one lakh. This method of random sampling involving adequate tools of behavioural science is used to arrive at probability percentage. No data conclusion is achieved without interacting with voters on the ground. Adequate representation of demography and caste is ensured. The model is based on primary data collection to predict voting choices and outcomes. It delves into behavioural science and uses quantitative data modelling to assign probabilities. We have used this methodology to predict the outcomes of a general election, a by-election and a state election many times before. I am personally on the ground with my team collecting data. I have travelled one lakh kilometres through 25 states in the last eight years. There is no secondary data collection.

This methodology has the ability to garner psephological and narrative feedback from the ground at the micro level. After many checks and balances, our model successfully captures the impact of political rallies held in constituencies. The following data shared in Figures 1, 2 and 3 is one example. It depicts the caste/community-wise shift on the three seats of Sambhal, Amroha and Moradabad following Prime Minister Modi's rally in Sambhal in west Uttar Pradesh on 19 February 2024.

Historically, despite many success stories of election surveys, the record is mixed. With the accurate prediction of the 2023 Mizoram elections, our tally stands at 39 and counting.

Figure 1

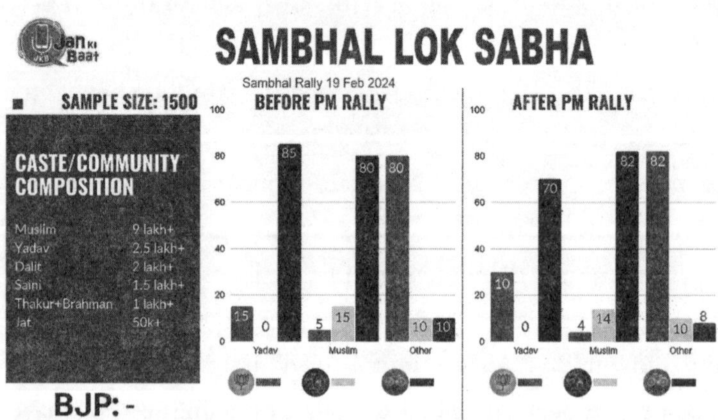

Figure 2

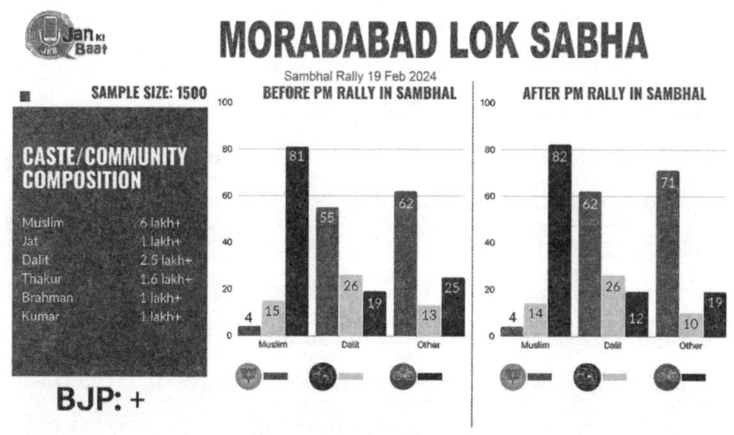

Figure 3

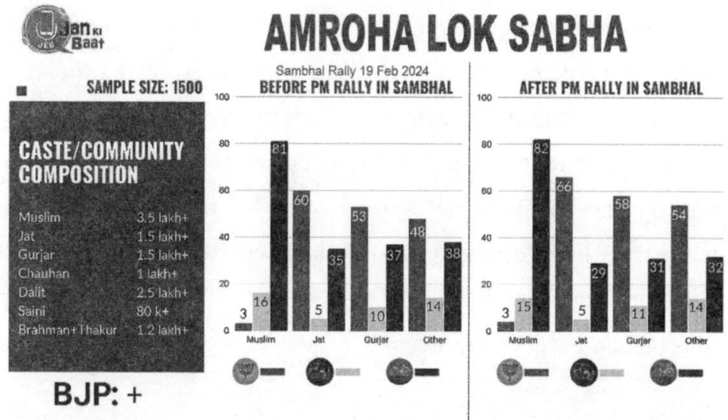

Indian General Elections: An Overview

Now let us take a minute to cast a mind's eye on the scale of this election—it is a marvel in itself. According to the Special

Summary Revision (SSR 2024), 96.88 crore registered voters will exercise their franchise this summer. The number is more than the population of Europe, and North and South Americas put together. This multitude of ordinary citizens, empowered with suffrage gifted by the Constitution, will decide the government for the next five years. There were 91.1 crore electors in 2019 and 83.4 crore in 2014. In the first general election of 1951, the electorate was only 17.3 crore. Despite that it was the largest democratic exercise conducted in the world. The 2024 elections will see 2.63 crore more first-time voters than 2019, which was around 1.5 crore, with women surpassing newly enrolled male voters by over 15 per cent, totalling around 1.41 crore. Male voters account for 46.4 crore while women stand at 43.1 crore. The Lok Sabha elections will be held in seven phases beginning from 19 April and the results will be announced on 4 June.

The staggering scale of Indian voters necessitates commensurate levels of polling wherewithal. Against 10 lakh polling stations in 2019 spread over 3.2 million sq. km of territory, the Election Commission will set up around 12 lakh polling stations to be managed by 1.5 crore polling officials and security staff.

Congress's Declining Fortunes: A Breakdown

As I write this chapter, two important developments have taken place which need to be mentioned. The Congress has stitched up deals with AAP in Delhi, Haryana, Gujarat, Goa and Chandigarh and with the SP in UP and Madhya Pradesh (MP). Let us analyse these.

Congress's Deal with AAP And SP

The Congress and AAP announced a 3–4 split in AAP's favour in Delhi. AAP will also contest Bharuch and Bhavnagar seats in Gujarat and Kurukshetra in Haryana. However, Punjab, where AAP is a key player, is not part of the deal. Even in states where Congress–AAP have deals, the question is whether there will be any complementarity, given AAP's small size in all but Delhi and given both parties' similar vote base.

Of bigger significance is the deal in UP where the SP will contest 63 seats and the Congress the remaining 17. But it will still be an uphill task. Prime Minister Modi will practically be on every BJP ticket with the party turning the polls into a referendum on him. Add to this BJP's successful targeting of OBC votes, including a small dent on the Yadavs, and it already has a formidable caste coalition in the state.

Kerala

The second interesting political event is that the INDIA bloc has crumbled in Kerala. The Communist Party of India (CPI), a partner of the ruling Communist Party of India (Marxist)-led Left Democratic Front (LDF) in Kerala, has nominated senior party leader Annie Raja, general secretary of the party's National Federation of Indian Women, as its candidate for the upcoming Lok Sabha polls from Wayanad, which is currently represented by former Congress president Rahul Gandhi. Besides Wayanad, the CPI has fielded its candidate Pannyan Raveendran from Thiruvananthapuram, another seat which is currently represented by the Congress leader, Shashi Tharoor. Despite being part of the INDIA bloc, the CPI and other Left parties are in a direct contest with the Congress-led United Democratic Front (UDF) in Kerala. This is a serious dampener for the Congress because Kerala is where it has a lot of hopes of doing very well. Speaking at a summit recently, Shashi Tharoor said, 'They (BJP) peaked in 2019. We are going to see nothing but a downward slide. How much downhill that is going to be depends on how effective the Opposition campaign is, which is just picking up (*The Hindustan Times*, 20 March).'

He may have to eat his words.

Delhi

Let us go back to the capital. Prior to the 2013 Delhi Assembly Elections, the BJP and the Congress were locked in a bipolar political contest here. Sheila Dikshit led the Congress to three consecutive electoral victories in the state, becoming the longest-serving chief minister of Delhi, as well as the longest-serving female chief minister of any Indian state (or UT). She served Delhi for a period of 15 years since 1998. Such was the combined popularity of the Left parties and the Congress that the latter got more than a 40 percentage vote share and more than 40 seats in 2008. Come 2013, the newcomer AAP, born out of Anna Hazare's anti-corruption agitation, played David to the Congress's Goliath and reduced the latter from more than 40 seats to eight seats in the 2013 Delhi Assembly.

AAP in its debut election got 28 seats, and Sheila Dikshit lost her seat to Arvind Kejriwal. It formed the state government after taking outside support from the Congress which allowed the government to last for only 49 days. This was not a political aberration. It was the beginning of a trend as far as Congress-inclusive alliances are concerned. In 2015, AAP swept the Assembly elections with 67 seats, and the Congress was literally wiped out. The Congress's vote share significantly dipped further.

In the 2020 Delhi Assembly Elections (Table 1), this trend persisted with AAP winning 62 seats, while the Congress could not even gather a single seat.

Table 1: Delhi State Assembly Elections Results (2013–2020)

Political Party	2013	2015	2020
BJP	31	3	8
INC	8	0	0
AAP	28	67	62

Source: Jan Ki Baat 2024 data analysis

The BJP's vote share remained constant between 2015 and 2018, plus minus 4 to 6 per cent (Table 2) because a large chunk of the Congress votes, and not the BJP's, shifted to AAP. Thus, it can be observed that the growth of AAP has not been at the cost of the BJP but the Congress, which has become a 'zero seat' party in Delhi.

Table 2: Overview of the Performance of AAP and BJP in Delhi Assembly Elections in 2015 and 2020

Party	AAP	BJP
2015 Elections	67	3
Seats won (2020)	62	8
Seat change	– 5	+ 5
Popular vote	4,974,592	3,575,529
Percentage	53.57%	38.51%
Swing	– 0.73%	+ 6.21%

Source: Jan Ki Baat 2024 data analysis

Table 3: Vote Share of the Delhi Lok Sabha in 2014 and 2019 (in percentage)

Constituency	Political Parties	2014	2019
Chandni Chowk	BJP	45	52
	INC	18	30
	AAP	30	14
	Others	7	4

Contd.

Northeast Delhi	BJP	45	54
	INC	16	29
	AAP	34	13
	Others	5	4
East Delhi	BJP	48	55
	INC	17	24
	AAP	31	17
	Others	4	4
New Delhi	BJP	47	54
	INC	19	27
	AAP	30	17
	Others	4	2
Northwest Delhi	BJP	46	60
	INC	39	21
	AAP	12	17
	Others	3	2
West Delhi	BJP	48	60
	INC	14	20
	AAP	29	18
	Others	9	2
South Delhi	BJP	45	57
	INC	35	26
	AAP	11	16
	Others	9	1

Source: Jan Ki Baat data analysis

In the 2019 Lok Sabha Elections, even if one added the vote share of the Congress and AAP together in each Lok Sabha constituency of Delhi, as seen above, the BJP was leading. The vote share of AAP in the 2019 General Elections has shrunk to just 18.1 per cent from 32.90 per cent in the 2014 Lok Sabha polls, with the party slipping to the third position in five of the seven constituencies. Therefore, if the BJP maintains its vote share tally of 2019, the INDIA bloc will not be able to win a single seat, provided the BJP changes candidates to ward off anti-incumbency. Undoubtedly, the BJP can accrue 50 per cent of votes on Prime Minister Modi's name in the Lok Sabha elections; however, its lack of a chief ministerial candidate who can challenge Arvind Kejriwal has been a big hurdle in Delhi. With Kejriwal in jail the INDIA bloc's Lok Sabha challenge in Delhi is in disarray.

One can analyse from the data presented above that the BJP's vote share from 2014 to 2019 has increased by at least 5 per cent.

I reiterate, when two parties who have always been antithetical to each other come in alliance, there is very little probability of the votes for the two parties to conflate. In fact, they reduce in number, and this is why the SP and the BSP alliance failed in UP, and this is why the AAP and the Congress alliance will fail in the 2024 Lok Sabha Elections. According to our analysis, the BJP is poised to win all the seats in Delhi. And this is not an isolated event but is reflected across the country. In contrast to the continuously downward spiralling trajectory of these anti-BJP alliances, the BJP has risen from a 2-seat party in Parliament in 1984 to a 303-seat party by 2019 and looks to be topping that number in 2024.

What then still tempts the INDIA bloc? To my mind, it is their belief in the saturation of the BJP vote share tally. In their minds, 2019 was when the BJP peaked and the bloc's combined vote share would be enough to defeat them this year. However, the BJP's vote share has increased overall nationally from 15 crore in 2014 to 22 crore in 2019. And Delhi was no exception where the vote share of the BJP increased from eight points, mid-40s to late 50s and early 50s. Our surveys on the ground have given a clear picture: Prime Minister Modi's popularity graph on the ground, irrespective of the geography, has only increased vis-à-vis 2019.

In contradiction to the INDIA bloc's calculations, the BJP could increase its vote share because of the transfer of the votes from the Congress and AAP on the ground where the workers may silently transfer their votes to the BJP to save their political fortunes.

Wins at the 2023 Assembly Elections in Three States

The BJP sweeping Rajasthan, MP and Chhattisgarh in the 2023 Assembly Elections was the writing on the wall for the

INDIA bloc. The verdicts exposed the soft underbelly of the Congress, of its ability to bargain for an advantageous seat sharing with other members of the alliance. Nitish Kumar, the *sootradharak* of the alliance, was first to sniff this weakness and dumped it. Others are extracting their pound of flesh by garnering more seats for themselves at the expense of the Congress.

The cross-voting in the 2024 Rajya Sabha polls by the SP and Congress MPs could very well be a trailer for what is to come. Seven MLAs of the SP have diverted from the party line and cross-voted for the BJP. There is now a possibility of the Congress losing the Raebareli seat as well. Today, the Congress faces a greater threat from its alliance partners than the BJP. The Congress's performance in the 2024 General Elections could be its nadir. As per our analysis, the Congress's seats could drop below 52 or around 2014 figures. Such an occurrence will definitely have ramifications on Indian politics at the national level.

Table 4: Congress Party's Performance in the Lok Sabha Elections of 2014 and 2019

Year	INC
2014	44 seats
2019	52 seats

Source: Jan Ki Baat data analysis 2024

Kerala and Punjab

The Congress procured 50 per cent of the seats in the 2019 Lok Sabha Elections from Kerala and Punjab. In Kerala, it got 15 seats and in Punjab it got 8. According to our findings, there is the possibility of at least 50 per cent depreciation in the seat tally of the party in Punjab and a minimum of 20 per cent in Kerala, *even in the best possible scenario.*

Table 5: Swing States to Decide the Congress Party's Performance in 2024

States	2019	2024
Kerala	15	80% – 3
Punjab	8	90% – 3

Source: Jan Ki Baat data analysis 2024

Conclusion: The negative swing of the Congress's vote probability – 80 per cent. Minimum negative swing of seats possible: 5 to 6.

So, the offset is a loss of five to six seats from these two states alone for the Congress, bringing their numbers down from the 2019 tally to 46 in 2024, which is just two more than 2014.

Raebareli, Uttar Pradesh

Raebareli Lok Sabha constituency in UP is a political powerhouse renowned for its significant influence in Indian politics. In the 2019 General Assembly Elections, it witnessed a fiercely contested battle. Sonia Gandhi won the election with a huge victory margin. She defeated Dinesh Pratap Singh of the BJP. However, the Jan Ki Baat Probability Map of Outcome predicts that there is 90 per cent probability that the Congress will lose Raebareli, particularly if Sonia Gandhi fights from there. If the BJP fields a strong candidate from there, there is a 90-percentage probability that the Congress can lose that seat, further bringing down their tally to 45. This scenario changes if there is a sudden surge in sentiments for the Gandhi family on the ground, but we do not foresee that happening. We see a shift of the SC voter from the Congress to the BJP in Raebareli this year.

Jharkhand and Chhattisgarh

Still staying with the Congress, let us discuss Jharkhand and Chhattisgarh. There are 14 Lok Sabha constituencies in Jharkhand. In the 2014 General Elections, the BJP had won 11 seats and the Congress one. There are 11 Lok Sabha constituencies in Chhattisgarh. In the 2014 General Elections, the Congress had won 2 seats and the BJP 9.

According to the Jan Ki Baat findings, there will be a drop of at least 50 percentage from both states for the Congress. Largely because the tribal votes are leaning towards the BJP. In Bastar, Chhattisgarh, the BJP got majority votes in the Assembly elections in 2023 unlike in the 2013 Assembly Elections when it was in power. There will be a dip in two seats possible from these two states, which takes the Congress tally from 45 to 43, which is less than 2014. And these are not the ideal-case scenarios.

In MP, the Congress has 50 per cent probability of retaining Chhindwara, bringing its tally down to 42. Here too the tribal vote is leaning towards the BJP.

Table 6: Swing in the Hindi Heartland States for the Congress

State	Swing Negative	Swing Positive	Seats change	Probability
Chhattisgarh	Negative		– 1	85%
Madhya Pradesh	Negative		– 1	75%
Rajasthan	None		–	85%
Jharkhand	Negative		– 1	82%
Uttar Pradesh	Negative		– 1	90%
Bihar			–	–

Source: Jan Ki Baat data analysis 2024

Conclusion: The Hindi heartland swing possibility for the Congress: – 4 seats.

Average probability to achieve it: 80 per cent.

In 2019, the Congress could get 52 seats because they won seats in MP, Jharkhand and Chhattisgarh, and from its earlier bastions of Kerala and Punjab it could sweep a majority of seats. The southern states—Tamil Nadu, Kerala, Karnataka, Andhra Pradesh and Telangana, and the Union Territory of Puducherry—send 130 MPs to the Lok Sabha. Out of the 52 Lok Sabha seats, the Congress won 28 from Kerala, Tamil Nadu, Telangana, Karnataka and Puducherry. The chances of retaining or gaining more seats are slim this time because more southern parties have formed alliances with the BJP, like the TDP–Jana Sena combine in AP, which brings the Kammas, to which TDP president N. Chandrababu Naidu belongs, Kapus, a community Jana Sena leader and actor Pawan Kalyan on the same platform. The alliance will get 10 to 14 seats.

Anti-incumbency may lead to the possibility of the Andaman and Nicobar Islands shifting from the Congress. Even Daman and Diu can shift away from the Congress, and the possible tally continues to slip further to 39.

Where Can the Congress Do Better?

The Congress has a chance of increments in Telangana and Karnataka. Although in Karnataka, the JD(S) and the BJP 28-seat sharing alliance may whittle down any substantial increase in seats for the party. There is a good possibility of a rise in seats in Telangana, but that will be a marginal increase of one to three seats, which still keeps the Congress at less than 44.

Table 7: Other States Where the Congress Swing Is Possible

State	Swing	Possibility
Assam	− 1	72%
Karnataka	+ 4 / − 1	74%
Telangana	+ 1	72%
Tamil Nadu	− 1 − − 2	76%

Source: Jan Ki Baat data analysis 2024

Overall negative swing: − 4 to − 5 seats, probability of this negative swing: 76 per cent.

Overall positive swing: + 3, probability to achieve this positive swing: 71 per cent.

The Congress could also get some seats in Maharashtra, Bengal (2) and Assam (3). However, our findings show that even here a dip of one or two seats is possible, which gets the Congress down to 37.

The Congress's Seat Share in the 2024 General Elections: Our Estimation

Therefore, it is likely that the Congress seat tally will be less than 40 in the 2024 General Elections. And it is certain that the Congress will get around 44 seats in this elections.

Table 8: Probability Scenario for the Congress in 2024

Congress	Minimum probability of the seat count happening
< 52 (2019 tally)	92%
< 44 (2014 tally)	75%

Source: Jan Ki Baat data analysis 2024

Why the Congress's Tally Could Go below 40?

Naturally, certain seats will only be decided very close to the election in the polling booth. And these pockets will all depend on how the momentum shapes, but what we can conclude with certainty is that the Congress will fall below the 2019 tally, and it is highly likely that it is can be less than the 2014 tally. And there is also 50 per cent likelihood that it will fall less than then 40 seats. Why do we say so? Because in the 17 Lok Sabha Elections under the DMK-Congress accord in Tamil Nadu, the Congress seat share was 9. If the alliance happens, the DMK will give the Congress fewer seats because it is weaker. This holds true with other members of the INDIA bloc. There is no pull factor in these states.

Needless to say, this is entirely the opposite scenario for the BJP.

Will the BJP Cross Its Previous Tally of 303 Lok Sabha Seats?

The BJP graph has since 2014 only shown an upward trajectory, while the Congress continues a downward trend. The BJP is poised to wrest most of the seats that the Congress is losing. The question which comes to mind is, will the BJP cross its previous tally of 303 Lok Sabha seats? The prime minister has set an ambitious target of 400 seats for the NDA with the BJP procuring more than 370. The BJP had won 282 and 303 of them in 2014 and 2019 respectively.

Prime Minister Modi has linked the target of 370 with the removal of Article 370 in the erstwhile Jammu and Kashmir. Addressing a meeting of the BJP's national office-bearers in February 2024, he said, '370 is not merely a number for the BJP. It symbolises a profound sentiment. (Syama Prasad) Mookerjee made the ultimate sacrifice for the abrogation of Article 370 to preserve our nation's unity and integrity. As a true tribute to him, the BJP should secure victory in 370 seats (*The Economic Times*, 18 March 2024).'

I think Prime Minister Modi is being very motivational by setting such ambitious targets as this will shake the workers out of complacency and get them motivated to work harder. Just as a CEO of a company drives his workers on with ambitious targets or as sportspersons set higher goals for themselves, the prime minister's vision of 400 for the NDA or 370 for the BJP must be looked from that point of view.

General Elections 2024: Key States Outlining the Road Map to Delhi

Uttar Pradesh

There is a saying that the road to Delhi goes through Lucknow, but this year it will need to pass through a few key states poised to host crucial contest that will shape the narrative in the days to come. Well, the road for the BJP to cross 303 will go from Uttar Pradesh. Can the BJP increase its tally in UP than what it was last time? Has it reached its saturation point? In 2014, the BJP–NDA in UP got 72 seats and the NDA in 2019 got 64 seats, despite the BSP–SP alliance. The vote share of the BJP rose from 42 per cent in 2014 to 49 per cent in 2019. The Jan Ki Baat Probability Map of Outcome Data indicates that the BJP, at the time of writing this chapter, is at its strongest in UP—aforesaid, even Raebareli can fall away from the Congress. A quick review of the many elements that will maintain or propel the NDA forward in UP are the positive mood of the people in favour of the Modi government; the economic transformation in the state that are reflected in, say, Varanasi in comparison to

Raebareli; the transfer of the BSP and the SP votes to the NDA; the ever-increasing popularity of Prime Minister Modi; and most importantly the building of the Ram Mandir in Ayodhya.

We may be looking at a BJP with a larger seat count in UP than in 2014 and certainly more than 2019. We forsee a minimum increment of 10 seats for the BJP in this year's general elections. Our analysis tells us that the INDIA bloc partners of SP and Congress will not raise their seat strength—and the Congress will draw zero in the state. The reader may recall that in the last Assembly elections in UP, of the 403 Assembly seats, Congress lost 401 and many Congress candidates lost their deposits in a majority of seats. This was despite Priyanka Gandhi Vadra being the face of the elections and the *ladki hun lad sakti hoon* campaign slogan.

Last time, the SP had the BSP to add some votes; this time, the SP has a 'zero party' like the Congress in the state as an alliance member. In fact, many core voters of the SP, that is, the Yadavs, will vote for the BJP. So, we are looking at a scenario where the BJP will increase its seats in UP by 10 with a more than 50 per cent vote share for the NDA. And the probability of that happenning according to us is at least more than 85 per cent. Thus, if everything else is constant, the BJP, which increased its overall tally from two seats in 1984 to 303 seats in 2019, is poised to get at least 315 or more than 310 in 2024.

Table 9: NDA Seat Tally Projection in Uttar Pradesh for 2024

	2014	**2019**	**2024**	**Probability**
Seat Share	72	64	Approx. 72 – 74	80%
Vote Share	42	49	Approx. 50 +	80%

Source: Jan Ki Baat data analysis 2024

The Other Hindi Heartland States

While the Uttar Pradesh seat tally has the advantage of bestowing a pole position to parties in any general election, other states also have significant impacts on the electoral landscape. Let us look at the other Hindi heartland states of MP, Rajasthan, Bihar and Chhattisgarh. In 2019, the BJP along with its allies not only bagged 165 out of 185 Lok Sabha seats, but also enjoyed a massive vote swing in its favour. We saw the party getting more than 90 per cent seats from this region and we do not see a significant dip happening here.

The Southern States

The 130 Lok Sabha seats in the south, Andhra Pradesh (25), Karnataka (28), Kerala (20), Tamil Nadu (39), Telangana (17) and Puducherry (1) were of special interest for the Jan Ki Baat team because of the many political noises about the alleged north–south divide. Our analysis is that the BJP will perform better than 2019 in terms of vote. In the last Lok Sabha polls, the Congress won 28 Lok Sabha seats from the south—Kerala (15), Tamil Nadu (8), Telangana (3), Karnataka (1) and Puducherry (1), while the BJP won 29 seats—Karnataka (25) and Telangana (4).

Telangana

We are anticipating that the BJP will increase its seat tally in Telangana with a minimum of three seats and the vote share will increase to more than 20 percentage. This is a good improvement over the 2019 Lok Sabha Elections. Its vote share rose from 4 per cent to 14 per cent in the last Assembly elections. The BJP is stronger than what it was and is now a dominant party vis-à-vis the Lok Sabha, overtaking the BRS and the Congress. In fact, when we had travelled on the ground in Telangana, our poll findings indicated that those who had voted for the Congress or the BRS in the Assembly elections will vote for Prime Minister Modi in the forthcoming general elections. If you remember the recent video of A. Revanth Reddy, the chief minister of Telangana, which went viral where he said to the public that they will give free bus rides and 2,500 rupees per month to women, grants to youth and farmers, etc., if they vote for the party in the Lok Sabha. The psephologist in me thinks that he is not confident of getting majority seats in the Lok Sabha, so as a political strategy he may field a Gandhi family member from the state. Whether or not that happens is to be seen. However, it is doubtful that such an event will wipe out the BJP from the state.

In summation, for the BJP there is an upward trend in Telangana with the probability of a minimum of three seats.

Tamil Nadu, Karnataka and Kerala

In Tamil Nadu, the BJP had no seats and only 2.5 and to 3 percentage vote share. This time round, the ground report tells us that the vote share will increase by a minimum of 14 percentage points. Also, there is an upward trajectory of seats even in Tamil Nadu for the BJP.

In Karnataka with the BJP–JD(S) alliance in place, the number of seats that the BJP will fight maybe lower—they might give three seats to the JD(S) but overall, the NDA will have no significant dip in the seat tally in the state. Andhra Pradesh will see no improvement in the BJP performance, but we can see it being an NDA-friendly state.

In Kerala at least one seat may go to the BJP, it is not a surety though.

So out of the five southern states, we will see the BJP performing marginally better or equal to what it had done in 2019. The probability of the BJP increasing its seats from the southern states is 54 percentage, but the probability of the number of seats decreasing from these states is less than 50 per cent. But there is little likelihood that the NDA will reduce its seats from the southern states combined than what it had got in 2019. So, the thinking that the BJP gains in UP will be offset by the southern states is not true.

Table 10: Vote Share of the BJP in Southern States in 2019 and 2024

	2019 seats	**2019 vote share %**	**2024 seats**	**2024 vote share %**
Telangana	4	19	7– 8	20 +
Tamil Nadu	0	2.5 – 3	1–3	14 +
Kerala	0	13	1	-------
Karnataka	25	51.38	Same as 2019	Same as 2019
Andhra Pradesh	0	0.98	2	-------

Source: Jan Ki Baat data analysis 2024

The probability of the BJP increasing its seats from the southern states is 54 percentage. There are strong chances that BJP will increase its seats and votes from the southern part of India.

Swing States for the BJP in the 2024 General Elections

Odisha

The three swing states of these elections are Maharashtra, Odisha and Bengal. Last elections, Odisha saw the BJP getting eight seats. This time as per our analysis and data, the BJP will emerge in the Lok Sabha (not in the Assembly, the elections for which will also be held during May–June 2024) as the dominant party in the state. There will be an increment of minimum four seats in Odisha. The Jan Ki Baat team had polled Chief Minister Naveen Patnaik's Assembly constituency of Hinjili and across the Ganjam district, his bastion.

As we stood in front of the statue of the late, great leader of Odisha, Biju Patnaik, we interacted with people assembled there. I started to collect data of women, youth and seniors; all three classes showed a 55 per cent upward trend for the BJP. Many said that they wanted Narendra Modi as the prime minister, but when we asked about Assembly elections their overall opinion was different. They wanted their beloved chief minister to continue. There was appreciation of the various benefits that they were accruing from the Centre, especially from people living in rural areas. This was not the scenario in 2019. We had covered the similar districts and saw a complete wave in favour of Naveen Patnaik.

In 2024, we anticipate a wave for Prime Minister Modi, even in a swing seat of Puri, which was won by Pinaki Misra of the BJD by a whisker; Sambit Patra of the BJP gave a very good fight. We see a swing of more than 49 percentage points towards the BJP in Puri in the 2024 Lok Sabha Elections. The BJP is making a dent in Naveen Patnaik's traditional stronghold. Its vote share will also increase across Odisha by at least 7 to 8 percentage, and by a minimum of four to five seats with a probability of 85 percentage.

Bengal

In the second swing state of Bengal, Mamata Banerjee has always won for the following three reasons: 1) the majority of women vote for her; 2) strong cadre at the polling booth; 3) minority vote and peak consolidation. Sandeshkhali is an inflection point in the politics of Bengal with genuine anger visible on the ground. Since January this year, the small Indian island near the Bangladesh border has been in the spotlight after a political storm broke out over allegations of corruption and sexual assault against the local leader Shahjahan Sheikh. We gather from the ground that women, in particular ST women, have expressed anger against him and particularly at the state government led by the TMC for shielding the accused. This gives an opportunity to the BJP to reflect the ground sentiment and bring unity. The swing factor allows for the BJP to procure 60 per cent women votes from 5.8 per cent of the ST and 23 per cent of the SC population. A bipolar scenario can help the BJP maintain 18 seats or go higher. The probability of this is 52 per cent and not 80 per cent. In the 2019 Lok Sabha polls, the TMC won 22 seats, the Congress 2 and the BJP 18. In Bengal, the variable factors till the time of polling and voting are more complex than any other state. It is said in Bengal only the public sentiment can make you win an election.

Maharashtra

Now come to the third very interesting state of Maharashtra which holds the second-highest number of Lok Sabha seats, 48, making it one of the centres of attraction during any Lok Sabha elections. Maharashtra is also a stronghold of some of the big national parties such as the BJP, the Nationalist Congress Party (NCP) and the Congress. The Shiv Sena fought side by side with the BJP in NDA against the Ajit Pawar-led NCP and the Congress in the 2019 General Elections, but in an unpredictable turn of events, the BJP will have support from both the Shiv Sena and the NCP, while still going up against both of the parties, as they have split. Shiv Sena is divided into Shiv Sena (Uddhav Thackeray) and Balasahebanchi Shiv Sena (Eknath Shinde), while the NCP is divided into NCP (Ajit Pawar) and NCP Sharadchandra Pawar (Sharad Pawar). To make things stranger, the newly formed Shiv Sena and the NCP will be a part of the NDA alliance, while the other Shiv Sena and the NCP will be a part of the INDIA alliance. In 2019, the Shiv Sena got majority of its votes in the name of Prime Minister Modi, not Uddhav Thackeray. It was Prime Minister Modi who had ensured that the Shiv Sena get up to a 15 to 20 percentage vote share.

This time, Thackeray is with the NCP but his large core voter base for the Lok Sabha is with the BJP. Thackeray's vote share is expected to dip by 15 to 20 percentage if it contests on the similar seats. Shinde will take a chunk of votes away from the Sena tally. In the battle between uncle and nephew Sharad Pawar and Ajit Pawar respectively, our data analysis suggests a 20 per cent vote in favour of the latter. This was the minimum split. We observe that there will be either a 50–50 split or a 70–30 split. The Ajit Pawar faction combined with the BJP offers a real challenge to the INDIA bloc in Maharashtra especially as there is no anti-incumbency regarding Prime Minister Modi. In the 2019 General Elections, the BJP had won 23 of the 25 seats, while its then alliance partner—the undivided Shiv Sena—won 18 of the 23 seats it had contested. This time the BJP is in a better position to fight on more than 25 seats, thereby having an opportunity to win more.

So, in the three swing states, there is certainty that the BJP seat tally is increasing.

Northeastern States

The northeastern states have the ability to affect the final result of the upcoming general elections as both national and regional parties fight for control. Arunachal Pradesh, Manipur, Meghalaya, Tripura, Mizoram, Nagaland and Sikkim may just have 1 or 2 seats each in their account but are significant collectively during any Lok Sabha election. Historically, regional parties have dominated the states, with national parties finding it difficult to establish their position. Nonetheless, the BJP has turned into a serious contender in the region. The BJP made Assam a cornerstone of its development in the northeast, and has also won the hearts and minds of the people from the other northeastern states in the spheres of education, healthcare, etc. The region has gone from an infrastructure deficit to an infrastructure surplus. This has been reflected in the increase in the NDA tally in the region from 2014 to 2019. The BJP's surge in the northeast, which began in 2014, continued with the saffron party and its allies winning in 17 of the 24 Lok Sabha seats in the region in the 2019 General Elections. In 2014, the BJP had bagged eight seats in the region, including seven in Assam. Tables 11–13 reflect the upward swing in seat share for the BJP, while Table 14 shows the negative swing in seat share.

Table 11: Swing States Probability (BJP)

	2024 Seat Prediction	**2019 seats**	**Probability 2024**
Maharashtra	Increase	23	82%
West Bengal	Increase by 4–5, 24–25 possible	18	45%
Odisha	+ 4–6	8	88%

Source: Jan Ki Baat data analysis 2024

Table 12: Swing States to Decide BJP Seats in the 2024 General Elections

States	Upward swing possible (minimum–maximum)	Probability to achieve it
Uttar Pradesh	8–24	87%
Odisha	4–7	90%
Maharashtra	1–4	62%
Tamil Nadu	0–3	70%
Telangana	2–4	74%
Madhya Pradesh	2	55%

Source: Jan Ki Baat data analysis 2024.

Table 13: States Where the Swing in the Seat Count Will Be Decided in the Last Minute

West Bengal	+ 1 – + 7	72%

Source: Jan Ki Baat data analysis 2024

In Bengal, there could be a positive swing scenario because of the following factors:

- Women vote for the BJP
- Free and fair polling machinery
- Polarization

Table 14: Negative swing scenario: 55 per cent women with the TMC, 90 per cent minority vote, vote machinery with the TMC, election booth capturing

West Bengal	– 6 to –3	52%

Source: Jan Ki Baat data analysis 2024.

Table 15: Other Swing States Analysis (Punjab, Himachal Pradesh, Haryana, Jharkhand, Chhattisgarh, Goa, Kerala, Andhra Pradesh, Gujarat, Assam, Karnataka, Northeastern States, Union Territories)

Overall swing	Positive / Negative	Probability of swing to achieve
Expected	Positive	83%

Source: Jan Ki Baat data analysis 2024.

Table 16: Class Vote Split in Tally in 2024 vis-à-vis 2019 for the BJP

Class of Voters	Swing Possible	Probability
Women	Positive	94%
Youth (18–40)	Positive	92%
Middle Aged (40–60)	Positive	82%
Elderly	Positive	97%

Source: Jan Ki Baat data analysis 2024

The quantity of votes for the BJP in 2024 can be more than 2019— probability 88 per cent.

Table 17: Class-wise Split in Voting 2024 vis-à-vis 2019 for the Congress

Class of Voters	Swing Possible	Probability
Women	Negative	68%
Youth (18–40)	Negative	69%
Middle Aged (40–60)	Constant	62%
Elderly	Negative	73%

Source: Jan Ki Baat data analysis 2024

Conclusion: The Congress vote remains stable or dropping compared to 2019—probability 70 per cent.

Table 18: Jan Ki Baat Vote Share Story Conclusion

Vote Share Swing	BJP	INC
Vote share swing 2019–2024	Positive	Negative or constant
Probability of achieving this vote share	94%	80%

Source: Jan Ki Baat data analysis 2024

Table 19: Caste-wise Swing Probability for the BJP

Caste Vote	Swing	Achieving Probability
SC	Positive	88%
OBC	Positive	83%
General	Positive	53%
Other caste / community	Positive	92%
Minority	Positive	58%

Source: Jan Ki Baat data analysis 2024

Table 20: Overall Caste-wise Split Probability for the Congress

Caste	Swing	Probability to achieve
SC	Constant / Negative	76%
OBC	Negative	85%
General	Negative	82%
Other Castes	Negative	84%
Minority	Constant	94%

Source: Jan Ki Baat data analysis 2024

Table 21: Southern States: A Probable Tally to Understand If North vs South Narrative Is True

States	Probability of BJP getting less votes than 2019	Probability of BJP staying constant as 2019	2019 more voter turnout
Kerala	12%	40%	48%
Karnataka	18%	52%	30%
Tamil Nadu	20%	10%	80%
Andhra Pradesh	13%	82%	5%
Telangana	31%	5%	92%

Source: Jan Ki Baat data analysis 2024

Conclusion: Overall, the BJP/NDA will get more votes in 2024 from southern states than in 2019.

Table 22: Narendra Modi Popularity Meter in 2024 (Region-wise vs 2019)

Region	Popularity Meter	Swing votes from 2019
Eastern states (West Bengal, Odisha, Northeastern States)	82%	Positive
Northern states and Western states	84%	Positive
Southern India (Andhra Pradesh, Kerala, Tamil Nadu, Telangana, Karnataka)	75%	Positive

Source: Jan Ki Baat data analysis 2024

Table 23: Northeast: Seat increase 2019–2024

	2019 Seats	2019%	2024 Seats Predicted
Assam	9	---	increase
Tripura	2	----	same
Manipur	2	----	same
Mizoram	2	5.57	same

Source: Jan Ki Baat data analysis 2024

Table 24. Probability of BJP's Seat Count in the 18th Lok Sabha

Number	Probability
Less than 272	32%
272–303	46%
More than 303	85%

Source: Jan Ki Baat data analysis 2024

Figure 4

Is NDA 400 possible?
Sample Size - One Lakh
Methodology - Probability Map Of Outcome Study through Random Sampling
Date - 22 February – 10 March
2019
8% Probability
less than 352
NDA 352
49% Probability
381 – 410 NDA
UP & Bihar   constant
Hindi heartland   constant
East   dip
South   dip
NDA 352-380
Odisha BJP-BJD alliance +13
UP   +12
Tamil Nadu   +2
Telangana   +4
Jharkhand   +1
Chhattisgarh   +1
Madhya Pradesh   +1
Kerala   +1
Bengal   +4
UP & Bihar   +ve
South   +ve
Hindi heartland   constant
East   constant
43% Probability
Andhra Pradesh   +15
(Friendly NDA alliance)
Conclusion
(As of 10 March 2024)
43% probability of NDA crossing 2019 tally of 352
49% probability of NDA touching 410
8% probability of NDA at less than 2019 tally of 352 seats

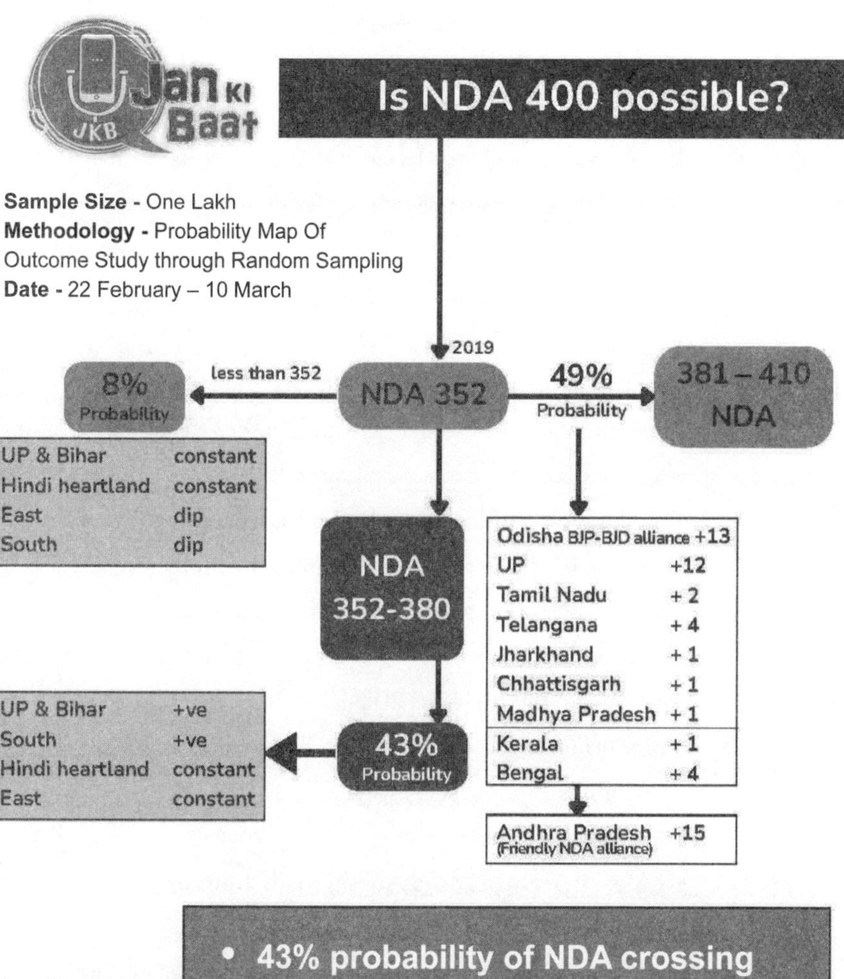

Conclusion

1. The BJP in 2024 can get more seats and votes than 2019 – 80 per cent probability.

2. The Congress will get lesser number of seats than 2019 – 80 per cent probability (Congress less than 50 seats).

3. More women will vote for Prime Minister Modi in 2024 than in 2019 – 84 per cent probability.

4. The BJP's performance in southern states will be better than 2019 – 80 per cent probability (in terms of post equality)

5. The Congress can lose their bastion Raebareli, which they held for three decades – 90 per cent probability (SC, ST, Brahmin, general votes shift to the BJP).

6. The top three parties of the Opposition to garner votes in double digits in 2024: DMK, INC, TMC, but will not touch the 50 seats tally. — 89 per cent probability.

7. The scenario changes if:
   - Vote percentage drops substantially from the 2014 and 2019 levels.
   - Situation can change from pro-Modi to anti-Modi due to Black Swan events…
     — 18 per cent probability.

Thus, in light of the aforesaid factors, the chances for the BJP to increase its seat tally to 303 or more this time is more than 80 per cent. It is a very bold prediction that I am making: the BJP will win more seats than it had in the 2019 General Elections. It will increase its vote share percentage across India, and this includes the big southern states. It is highly likely that the Congress's seat share will drop below 52 seats.

In Bihar the NDA will retain around the same number of seats they held in 2019, that is, 39 seats. In 2024, I estimate that there is 90 per cent probability of the NDA reaching its 2019 tally; it could probably go up to 40. This percentage holds true even if Nitish had remained with the INDIA bloc. The NDA would have got majority seats even in that scenario. The BJP is not only fighting to win this election, but also to maximize its seat count and vote count. In Punjab too, the BJP will see some addition in seat share.

Now let us look at the incremental gains or losses for the BJP in Tamil Nadu. This year, Tamil Nadu also could see an upward trajectory for the BJP as compared to 2019. The BJP will dominate Assam, perhaps more than 2019. Therefore, the probability for the BJP to maintain its record number of 9 seats in Assam is 98 per cent and for it to increase its seat count marginally by one or two is at least 84–85 percentage. Again, if you look at the northeastern states of Manipur, Mizoram, Assam, Arunachal Pradesh, Meghalaya, Nagaland and Tripura, the tally of BJP will be roughly around what it had got last time. Despite the unfortunate violent clashes in Manipur, and so many lives lost, the BJP will retain its number of seats.

When I look at the map of India, I conclude that there is more than a 90 per cent probability that the BJP seat count will be more than what it was in 2019. This prediction can only go wrong if the party gets wiped out from one large state, like UP, Bihar, Maharashtra, Bengal or Odisha. The probability of the BJP being wiped out from the above states is 9 per cent. I do not see this happening. For the NDA to cross 400, it must sweep two new states than what it had in 2019 or forge two new alliances which can help it sweep two new states.

Many talk about caste-wise voting but in a wave election class-wise votes (women, youth, elderly) are important. I say this with conviction that Prime Minister Modi has moved India away from caste-dominated politics to caste-representative politics and developmental–surplus politics. At the heart of this development has been *nari shakti*. Prime Minister Modi has made politics gender neutral with women voters leading the fate of the Indian electorate. In a polling by Jan Ki Baat, women voters favour the prime minister for a third term with numbers as high as 80 per cent. This gives the BJP an advantage in many seats with a close margin and helps it win non-traditional geographies. No other political party or leader has been able to create even a minor dent in the support of the women voting class. Women support Prime Minister Modi with a loyalty factor as high as 90 per cent. This is why the final tally of the BJP even in 2019 crossed many expectations, and this support is more now than it has been in the past.

Analysing its class perspective goes hand in hand with the other two classes, that is, the youth and the elderly voter. Even in the elderly class, most of whom have lived their adult lives in the UPA era, most voters support Modi and cannot align themselves with the leadership of the Congress. They are solidly behind the prime minister as they were in the past.

For first-time voters it is not welfare that drives them to choose their leaders, it is the 'aspirational quotient'. They see Prime Minister Modi as a leader who has enhanced the prestige of India. For them no other Opposition leader comes close. These make the prime minister the first choice for the youth, with 60 per cent wanting him to return for a third term. With more than 60 per cent support in all three of these voting classes—the youth, elderly and women—no caste-based factor can overpower their choices in deciding the voting outcome and the tally for 2024. A random sampling of the classes makes this a 'jumbo' election rather than a normal election.

Towards this end, it is important to talk about the Muslim vote. Jan Ki Baat's sample set of the community points to a new trend. Despite the popular narrative, 65 per cent of those spoken to agree that Prime Minister Modi will return with a thumping majority. This was not the case in 2019 when only 22 per cent of the members of the community thought Prime Minister Modi would return. Our survey does not cover the trend of voting of the community in Kerala and Tamil Nadu. This does not necessarily mean that they will vote for the BJP, but it does mean that a community that has been a non-BJP voter also acknowledges the rise of Modi's popularity and 88 per cent of them said that they have not experienced *bhed-bhav* on receiving welfare benefits. To conclude from the behavioural science analysis, Narendra Modi 3.0 will be stronger and bigger. Only a political black swan event can change this.

4

The Modi Phenomenon

Unboxed

'Prime Minister Modi's charisma and chemistry make him tower over the present pantheon of leaders in India.'

To anchor the continuous rise of India's 14th Prime Minister Narendra Modi to the traditionalist constituency would be a limited understanding of the Modi Phenomenon. Many people aligned with colonialism and neocolonialism find it difficult to identify with native traditions, culture and philosophy, often displaying a tendency to sneer at the lack of 'sophistication' exhibited by people from the grassroots level. Hence, there is a great unmasked disdain for Narendra Modi; this is a blinkered look of what the reality is on the ground.

Narendra Modi's Politics of Hope

India has seen widely popular national leaders before, but many of them belonged to the privileged class. In contrast, Prime Minister Modi's rise is a bottom-up phenomenon—he belongs to a humble family background. Narendra Modi has famously said, 'The real strength of a democracy is at the grassroots levels.' Thus, he remains connected to the ground. The daily life for the common man is a constant struggle to survive and therefore they greatly appreciate the fact that the prime minister has climbed the political ladder on his own steam. He did not inherit his position. Hard work and grit were the multipliers here, *not the privilege of a famous surname.*

After meticulously toiling as a BJP party worker across the length and breadth of the country for many years, he became the 14th chief minister of Gujarat in 2001—a state he governed successfully for almost thirteen years. The Modi Phenomenon has many aspects which every Bhartiya relates to: struggle, hope and desire to achieve which resonate with the common man in this country. He has built an original thought process of looking at the country through his country-wide travels over decades in various capacities. This incredible man displays immense self-belief and has a remarkable sense of purpose in life.

Therefore, the fundamental appeal of Narendra Modi in contemporary India is not along the lines of religion or caste or even hyper-nationalism as many so-called political pundits would like us to believe. Born on 17 September 1950 in Vadnagar, a small town in North Gujarat, he is a self-made man whose father sold tea at a railway station and whose mother washed dishes at the houses of people to pay his school fees. This is an arresting and powerfully emotive chronicle. The entire family lived in a small single-storey house, which was approximately 40 foot by 12 foot.

For Prime Minister Modi being a *chaiwallah* (teaseller) is a badge of honour.

Prime Minister Modi is best known for his vision, immense capacity to work hard, firm-decision making ability and many incredible achievements. He is one of the longest-serving heads of elected government in India. He has never lost an election. He is the first prime minister who was born in independent India. He is a moderniser whose vision is to build a modern nation based on heritage, tradition and economic prosperity. After many decades since Independence, India has seen in Narendra Modi, a politically astute and extremely articulate leader with the potential to profoundly transform the country. In 2014, India responded to Modi's appeal and voted him to power. His victory in 2019 was even more impressive. The last time that a political party secured such an absolute majority was in the 1984 General Elections, but it was a sympathy vote. (The elections were a landslide victory for the Congress of Rajiv Gandhi, which won 404 of the 514 seats and a further 10 in the delayed elections.) Today, Prime Minister Modi stands like a colossus in the Indian political spectrum. He has launched super successful welfare schemes like Ayushman Bharat, UJALA and has gone out of his way to ensure '*Sabka Saath, Sabka Vikas, Sabka Vishwas*'. Prime Minister Modi has ushered in a paradigm shift in governance that has led to inclusive, development-oriented and corruption-free governance.

Narendra Modi's Core Voter Base

When history is ready for a change in its trajectory, things happen organically. Nurtured by his grassroots, Modi grew as India's one of the most powerful and popular leader and has held centre stage of Indian politics with the support of three main classes—the youth, women and the poor.

Youth

'The world sees the capability of Indian youth. Trusting their capabilities, we decided to fuel their aspirations. We have transformed people's thinking; instead of being a job-seeker, the youth is now keen on becoming a job-provider.'—Prime Minister Modi, *The Print*, 20 March 2024

Prime Minister Modi has touched the imagination of the youth. India has the largest working-age population in the world in the first half of the twenty-first century. The 2014 election was also the first for those born after the 1991 economic reforms. Modi's winning over the young voters even from communities that had hitherto been hostile to his party is a game changer. Since 2014, the young voters are particularly strong supporters of the BJP, and the party has diligently wooed this segment by initiating several programmes.

Narendra Modi started focusing on the youth much before the 2019 General Elections and urged them to register as voters. In his 2017 Independence Day speech, Prime Minister Modi said, 'They (the youth) are going to be the creators of the destiny of our nation in the twenty-first century. I heartily welcome all these youth, honour them and offer my respects to them. You have an opportunity to shape the destiny of our country. A proud nation invites you to become a part of its developmental journey.'

The BJP is extremely aware of the power of the vote of the youth and the prime minister has already successfully harnessed it in the past two general elections. A few months ago, he extended an invitation to the youth to contribute to the BJP's manifesto for the 2024 Lok Sabha Elections.

On the occasion of National Voters' Day in 2024, the prime minister 'guaranteed' the first-time voters that 'their dreams are his resolve' and encouraged them to be a part of the key democratic exercise. Notably, a day before, he had called the new generation—known as Gen-Z—as 'Amrit Peedhi (golden generation)'.

Women

'Our government is committed to empowering women through initiatives in education, entrepreneurship, agriculture, technology and more. This is also reflected in our accomplishments in the last decade.'— Prime Minister Narendra Modi's post on X on International Women's Day 2024

The second element in the Modi phenomenon is the women voter. Across India, notably in the Hindi heartland, women are voting in higher numbers, thus gradually bridging the gender gap in the voter turnout. Women voters are increasingly getting recognized as a constituency that can influence outcomes. If men vote on ideology, women vote on the tangibles—practical benefits that their families will enjoy.

Understanding this psyche, the Modi government has developed many women-centric schemes and successfully implemented them. A few of these initiatives are the Pradhan Mantri Ujjwala Yojana, which provided gas cylinders and gas stoves to 9.6 crore women; Jan Dhan Yojana which has 48 crore beneficiaries out of which 27.8 crore are women; Pradhan Mantri MUDRA Yojana (PMMY) which disbursed over 27 crore loans to women entrepreneurs; and POSHAN Abhiyaan which has significantly achieved improvement in nutritional status of children from 0–6 years, adolescent girls, pregnant women and lactating mothers in a time bound manner, reduced stunting and wasting in children (0–6 years) as well as reduced anaemia in women, children and adolescent girls.

The Beti Bachao Beti Padhao (BBBP) scheme was launched on 22 January 2015 with an aim to address declining child sex ratio (CSR) and related issues of empowerment of girls and women over a life cycle continuum. The objectives of the scheme are to prevent gender-biased sex-selective elimination, ensure survival and protection of the girl child and enable education and participation of the girl child.

The Swachh Bharat Mission was launched on 2 October 2014 to protect the dignity of women, and the Jal Jeevan Mission reduced women's problems with fetching drinking water in rural areas. Furthermore, Pradhan Mantri Awas Yojana Gramin (PMAY-G) provided homes to over 1.7 crore women, with women owning over 70 per cent of the PMAY households either solely or jointly.

Women have backed the BJP in 2019 and will continue to do so in 2024. Under these women-centric schemes, women have received the promised benefits, so they trust Prime Minister Modi. It is as simple as that.

The proposal to reserve 33 per cent seats in the Lok Sabha and state assemblies is a gender-justice step that the Modi government will highlight during the 2024 election campaign as it had done with the triple talaq ordinance before the 2019 polls. The ordinance was aimed at providing justice to the Muslim women.

The Poor

'I come from a poor family and I want the poor to get dignity.'—Prime Minister Narendra Modi's maiden Independence Day speech (*Hindustan Times*, 15 August 2014)

The upliftment of the poor is at the core of Prime Minister Modi's reforms. The 2023 Global

Multidimensional Poverty Index report states that India has registered remarkable reduction in poverty with 41.5 crore people coming out of it in 15 years (from 2005/2006 to 2019/2021).

Aggressive government efforts to alleviate multiple factors of poverty, such as improving access to food, fuel and electricity have greatly helped in achieving this stupendous outcome. The report commenting on the state of poverty around the world calls this 'a spectacular achievement by a young democratic nation'. The report adds that deprivation has declined in India, and 'the poorest states and groups, including children and people in disadvantaged caste groups, had the fastest absolute progress'. It further states, 'India was among the 19 countries that halved their global Multidimensional Poverty Index (MPI) value during one period—for India; it was 2005/2006, 2015/2016' (*Business Today*, 11 June 2023). The following nine schemes initiated by the Modi government have definitive progressive foundations.

- Har Ghar Jal (Jal Jeevan Mission);
- Har Ghar Shauchalay (Swachh Bharat Mission);
- Har Ghar Bijli (Saubhagya Yojana);
- Har Ghar Gas Cylinder (Ujjwala Yojana);
- Har Ghar Ration (Garib Kalyan Yojana);
- Har Ghar Bank Account (Jan Dhan Yojana);
- Har Ghar Swasthya (Ayushman Bharat Yojana);
- Har Ghar Teeka (Largest Vaccine Drive);
- Har Ghar Pakka Ghar (Pradhan Mantri Aawas Yojana).

The aforementioned schemes have transformed the lives of the poorest of the poor, raised their standard of living, which was curtailed by an inefficient delivery mechanism. Most importantly, these schemes serve the poor across every community, class, caste and gender divide.

Prime Minister Modi has been working persistently for the greater social cause. In January 2024 he said, 'True secularism and social justice mean when the government ensures that the benefits of its welfare schemes reach all the needy people without any discrimination and corruption … In Ayodhya, I said "pran pratishtha" has been completed; now it is time to take "rashtra pratishtha' to new heights" (*Business Standard*, 21 March).'

The Phenomenal Narendra Modi: Unravelled

Thus, Narendra Modi is more than a leader. He is a phenomenon. Look at Mamata Banerjee for example, her appeal is limited to the Bengali-speaking population in Bengal and she has not been able to evolve her party's graph beyond the state's borders. Or M.K. Stalin who simply cannot attract votes out of Tamil Nadu.

Narendra Modi's language of development and progress resonates with even those who do not speak the languages that he speaks. Tamil is not his first language, Telugu is not his first language. Neither Bengali is his first language, nor is Odia. Despite this, his political graph is increasing which tells you that this leader is connected to the hearts of the people. And when a leader connects to the hearts and the minds of the masses, the results show in the polls. Prime Minister Modi once said, 'I am a worshipper and the people are my god.'

Those in power who have kept a distance from the hearts and the minds of the common man cannot understand why Narendra Modi has surpassed all political expectations. Or what the Modi Phenomena is.

One of the biggest mistakes that the Opposition makes is to truly believe their own preconceived perceptions about the brand of politics. They consider that Prime Minister Modi pursues the communal and majoritarian. His second term win should have driven home the message that he is no fluke.

In essence, what is working for him is just not an ideological or a welfare factor. It is just not an aspirational factor. It is a composite of all of the above and more—everything what Bharat is about. It represents the civilizational glory—*virasat;* it entails hunger for development which every youth of this country wants.

Prime Minister Modi has been successfully establishing the base to sustain this hunger. When he was the chief minister of Gujarat for two decades, he spectacularly bulked up its economy with his policies. Although his governance model of Gujarat was ridiculed by many, yet this was what aspirational India hungered for. Hence he keeps returning to the Centre, and the country grows and prospers. Today we are the fifth-largest economy in the world (*Forbes India*, 7 February) and are well on the way to take the third spot by 2027 (*Hindustan Times*, 22 March 2024).

But Prime Minister Modi's impact runs deeper than material achievements. India has a rapidly growing economy and has set its sights on a grand ambition: to transform from a developing nation into a fully developed one. As India moves towards higher economic stature, its global stature too has risen. In a short span of a decade, the prime minister has raised the global profile of India. His firm handling of security issues and implementation of 'India First' policy—placing national interest above conventional geopolitics—has no doubt propelled India as one of the leading global powers. The citizens, including the man on the street, are aware of these developments and feel immensely proud of the prime minister's way of handling both global and national issues.

Allow me to quote from an article on the BBC website which reflects the mood of the voter in Kolkata on 29 May 2019: 'Modi is keeping the nation secure and keeping India's head high.'

The opinion on the streets has pretty much remained the same.

Therefore, the Opposition is simply unable to bring him down politically despite their best efforts. In their enthusiasm to defeat the BJP, Opposition leaders are making it very easy for Prime Minister Modi to convert the next election into a referendum on him. Their personal attacks on someone who has been voted as the most popular leader in the country in several surveys over the years, have cost them dearly in the past. And will do so in 2024. Rahul Gandhi's slur of *'chowkidar chor hai'* cost the Congress dearly in the 2019 General Elections. Rahul used this slogan to launch the attack on the Modi government on the Rafale deal. Prime Minister Modi turned around the slogan to his advantage. He would often call himself a 'chowkidar' and underline that he is working tirelessly to safeguard their interests. And thus reduced the Congress to 52 seats in the 2019 General Elections.

Well, not learning from history has dire consequences. Recently, Lalu Prasad Yadav hit back at the prime minister's charge of dynasty politics against many Opposition parties, including the RJD, by mocking that Narendra Modi has 'no family'. *Bad move*! Responding to the RJD patron's taunt, Prime Minister Modi said in a speech at a rally in Telangana recently that the people of the country 'consider me their own … love me like a member of their family … And that is why I say 140 crore people of this country are my family. The youth … crores of daughters, mothers and sisters … all the poor people in the country, they are my family. The millions of children and elderly in the country are Modi's family. Those who have no one belong to Modi and Modi belongs to them. My Bharat, my family (*The Indian Express*, 5 March 2024).'

Soon after, top leaders of the government started adding, 'Modi ka parivar' to their social media handles in solidarity with the prime minister. The widespread adaptation of the slogan by BJP leaders on social media had its desired impact and amplified the counteroffensive. Well, as someone famous once said: 'Those who fail to learn from history are doomed to repeat it.'

Now the BJP prime ministerial candidate for the 2024 Lok Sabha is getting reassurances from across India that they are his family. People at the rally in Telangana chanted, 'We are your family.' The timing of the slogan could not have been more perfect. By emphasizing a familial connection with the people, the BJP aims to strengthen its appeal and create a positive perception of Narendra Modi as a leader who belongs to everyone.

The BJP is a highly efficient organization led by a very capable captain. His persona has become larger than his cadre-based party, and a symbol of hope and aspiration for many. Under Modi, the BJP has developed into an efficient party machine, it has become the dominant party in India's crowded politics.

When a leader works round the clock, sometimes even 18 hours a day; when he attends a political meeting which last till 3:45 in the night, addresses a public rally at 7:30 the next morning and gives a lecture on governance to another crowd that very evening; that tells you something about the work ethic of the leader. Along with that, it also tells you his capacity to get flawless execution from his team in all aspects of governance. This leader has delivered on national security, which is second to none; he has delivered on grave issues like Article 370 without a single bullet being fired; and has delivered on civilizational issues like the Ayodhya Ram Mandir without a single riot. As they say, '*Modi hai toh mumkin hai* (it's possible if Modi is there).' He prioritizes execution and because what good is an idea if it is not implemented.

He has his vision for 2047 ready despite the general elections around the corner. In March 2024, he chaired a meeting where the council of ministers brainstormed on the vision document for Viksit Bharat 2047 and detailed action plan for the next five years. The goal is to transform India into a developed country by 2047, which marks the 100th year of independence. This vision covers various aspects like economic growth, social progress, environmental sustainability and good governance. At the BJP's national convention in February 2024, the prime minister called on the *karyakartas* to work with 'new energy, enthusiasm, belief' for the next 100 days for the Lok Sabha campaign. While workers were chanting '*ab ki baar 400 par*', the prime minister reiterated that the party has to cross the 370 mark. He is known to set high targets to motivate his colleagues and workers.

Why Is Narendra Modi an Unequalled Leader?

Prime Minister Modi's charisma and chemistry make him tower over the present pantheon of leaders in India. The following factors add to the Modi magic:

Visionary Leadership

Prime Minister Modi possesses a crystal-clear vision of how India's future will be. Viksit Bharat outlines his government's action plan to transform India into a developed country by 2047. The vision encompasses various aspects of development, including economic growth, social progress, environmental sustainability and good governance, among others. The prime minister has urged the citizens to take a pledge, 'Whatever I do should be for a developed India.'

Be it a goal of achieving a trillion-dollar economy, ease of doing business, increase in global export percentage or share in the global GDP, all the goals have been clearly stated and are being zealously pursued. The Indian economy is now one of the fastest-growing economies in the world. According to the data released by the Ministry of Statistics and Programme Implementation, its gross domestic product (GDP) grew at 8.4 per cent in the December quarter of 2023 (*Business Today*, 29 February 2024). India is experiencing all-round development of roads, public buildings and infrastructure sector at an unparalleled pace. The current regime is focussing on creating transparency, which is reflected in Digital India. Digital payment transactions have significantly increased as a result of coordinated efforts of the government as a whole, along with all stakeholders concerned, from 2,071 crore transactions in the financial year 2017–18 to 8,840 crore transactions in the financial year 2021–22 (Press Information Bureau, 8 February 2023).

Who could have imagined India celebrating drone festivals?

Valuing Indian Civilizational Ethos

Prime Minister Modi wears his pride for India's civilization on his sleeve, never missing an opportunity to project the values of Indian culture on any global platform. He has been relentless in his focus on Indian cultural roots and national values while understanding the needs of the nation in international affairs. During the 95th edition of *Mann Ki Baat* on 27 November 2022, the prime minister said that India is home to the oldest traditions in the world. Therefore, it is the citizen's responsibility to preserve its traditions and traditional knowledge, promote it and take it forward as much as possible. He gifts the Bhagavad Gita to visiting dignitaries, he invites people to visit India, he showcases Indian culture, like the Ganga Aarti, Sabarmati Ashram, temples of the south, to visiting heads of state. He is reviving Indian culture through temple resurrection, be it the reconstruction of the Ram Temple or Kashi Vishwanath, or other temples.

Decisive Leadership

India has not seen a more decisive and proactive leader in its history. His steely decision to sanction a surgical strike, ban triple talaq and abrogate Article 370 have forced even his hard critics to admit that he is a strong-minded leader.

Immense Personal Charisma

Narendra Modi's grit, steely determination and a tremendous capacity for hard work is topped by unparalleled eloquence. He understands the masses because of his humble background. Throughout his rich political career, not a single allegation of corruption has been levelled against him. As someone rightly said, for Narendra Modi, politics is not power but service. A rare quality that has only added to his popularity and vote-gathering ability.

Nehru and Modi: Representing Two Opposing Ideas of India

Prime Minister Modi's popularity is unmatched and incomparable. India's first prime minister Jawaharlal Nehru governed India for 17 years, and Prime Minister Modi too is all set to step into his third term. Seen as two of the most influential Indian prime ministers, comparisons are inevitable. However, comparisons are possible only at the superficial level because they both come from such different moulds.

For a start, both represent two opposing ideas of India.

Jawaharlal Nehru saw India's future through a Western prism. He fought for the independence of India but was dismissive of her ancient past, ignoring her deep cultural and civilizational wisdom, equating it with ritualism, superstition and prejudice.

In contrast, Prime Minister Modi's vision for India's future emerges from these very same cultural and civilizational wisdom.

Jawaharlal Nehru's elite background allowed him to step into the highest echelons of Indian polity effortlessly. Narendra Modi rose from poverty to the pinnacle of power without any dynastic patronage and through toil. He was a *pracharak* for thirty years, chief minister for 12 and a half years and has now almost completed 10 years as the prime minister.

Jawaharlal Nehru pinned an alien understanding of secularism on India and was overly protective of minorities, as if this ancient abode of Hindus would forget its culture of tolerance. Narendra Modi governs on the twin principles of dharma and development.

Jawaharlal Nehru discouraged President Rajendra Prasad from inaugurating the renovated Somnath Temple. Narendra Modi performed the prana pratishtha ceremony at the Ayodhya Shri Ram Mandir with the world's eyes on him.

Jawaharlal Nehru's irresolution led to the disastrous 1962 war with China. Narendra Modi's resolve resulted in the 2019 Balakot airstrike and the abrogation of Article 370. I could go on.

The fact is that when Jawaharlal Nehru took up the reins only 18.3 per cent of the population was literate. India's population today is 75 per cent literate and hence by far more aspirational (*Times of India*, 14 August 2022). Narendra Modi addresses a far more politically savvy electorate. Being an eloquent speaker and brilliant communicator adds to his great ability to connect with the masses.

When Jawaharlal Nehru was the prime minister, Jan Sangh was in its nascent stage. This is not the case today. Narendra Modi had to face an Opposition which was in power for seven decades.

The huge mandate for the Congress in the1984 General Elections was a sympathy vote. The one in 2024 will be a vote for good governance.

In my opinion, there is no comparison between the two leaders—Narendra Modi stands head and shoulders above Jawaharlal Nehru.

5

Indian Polity

The Way Forward

'Only a conscious, committed, nationalist and dharmic Opposition can take on the BJP.'

Amidst a challenging global scenario, India has emerged as a significant economic and geopolitical power. Its actions in the coming year could lay the groundwork for the country to become the world's third-largest economy in the next five years and a developed nation by 2047, setting an example on inclusive, sustainable economic growth; digital development and climate action.'

—World Economic Forum Annual Meeting,
15 January 2024

India is finally moving towards her rightful place in the sun—she stands on the cusp of major change: a transformation from an underdeveloped to a developed nation, with a surging economy, commitment to inclusivity, sustainability and international cooperation. Merely a decade ago, the idea of India becoming a developed country in the near future seemed a distant reality. Since then, however, there has been a sea change in her own and the world's perception about her future. For a nation to rise, there must be a calibrated interface between politics, economics and governance, for it is their combined effect on the functioning of our democracy which will largely determine India's future.

Evolution of the Indian Polity

After Independence, many political, social and economic transformations have taken place in India. Today, under the leadership of Prime Minister Modi there is a political will to seize opportunities that will push us towards the goal of becoming a developed nation.

This era is also witnessing a changing Indian democracy at the national, regional and local levels of politics. By reconnecting polity to its roots, the Indian political scene has transformed at various levels. Indian politics used to, by and large, be driven by the two Cs—caste and communal politics. As our democracy began stretching and looking inwards for its essence, the Indian voter's psyche also began pulling away from dominant caste and communal politics.

In 2014, Prime Minister Modi changed this baseline of the polity to the two Ds—dharma and development. For the first time since Independence, the Indian polity has changed from being Congress-dominated to being Bhartiya Janta Party-dominated.

Decline of the Congress

The Election Commission has withdrawn the national party status of the TMC, the NCP and the CPI. The BJP, Congress, CPI (M), BSP, National People's Party (NPP) and AAP are recognized as national parties, with the BJP and the Congress leading in seat and vote shares. Will the Congress hold its position as leader of the Opposition?

If the Congress falls less or even gains a handful more seats than its 2019 tally, this will be its third successive defeat under the leadership of Sonia Gandhi, Rahul Gandhi and Priyanka Gandhi Vadra. Given the nature of the party, the continuous deluge of party leaders is inevitable. This necessitates the question: how much longer can the Gandhi family survive? They have their diehard loyalists who insist that come what may, the family is the glue that holds the Congress together.

So, could there be a split in the party in the aftermath of the general elections?

This 18th Lok Sabha Elections is an existential one for the Gandhi family more than the Congress. It presents yet another opportunity for the party to reinvent itself. If it does not, it may be too late.

Prime Minister Modi understands that the youth of India want development to be the driving force of policies. Hence his governance agenda is all about development and reforms. The Congress and their allies need to present concrete measures that they would take for the country to continue its forward trajectory. If they continue on the same path, they will soon become irrelevant—the signs are there for all to see. Even after the predictable outcome of the 2024 General Elections, if the Congress continues to remain under the leadership of the Gandhi family, even God cannot save it.

As I write this chapter, reports are coming in that Rahul will be fielded from Wayanad yet again. He may not contest from Amethi, while the suspense is on whether Priyanka will be contesting from Raebareli—Sonia's bastion—remains. This smacks of a lack of confidence in the leadership of the family.

Ever since Narendra Modi became the prime minister, he has rendered the party that governed the country for more than 50 years to a political fringe, which cannot even stake leadership of the INDIA bloc with confidence. This is why I call this a watershed election, for it will decide the state of the Opposition, whether the Congress will be able to shake off the Gandhi family and split. If the family retains their hold, it will no longer remain a mainstream party.

Emergence of the New Indian Voter

The Indian voter today looks for three things in any political party:

- the leader of the party stands with the poor and is focused on improving their life;
- the party is sensitive and respectful of the dharmic traditions/Sanatan Dharma;
- it is not a family-run enterprise.

A Shift from Caste-Dominated to Caste-Representative Politics

The electorate will not tolerate arrogance in any public representative. Good governance and respect for Sanatan Dharma are what the voter wants over caste- and communal-based politics. Focusing only on the two Cs will not work anymore because the country has shifted from caste-dominated polity to caste-representative polity. Neglecting to hear the voice of the majority community and expecting to win is a thing of the past. Today the Hindus are no longer apologetic about following their traditions.

Traditional Votebanks Are Shrinking

Additionally, the political scene has become more of a bipolar contest. The Congress, the 'Mandal' parties and the Left—the traditional parties, each representing a distinct ideological space that covered the political space post-Independence—are in deep crisis in the present era of BJP dominance. Further, during the period between 1996 and 2014, state-based parties were essential to the creation and survival of all national-level governments; they even led two federal governments, had key ministerial portfolios in coalition governments and had a greater say in decision making at the national level. From a position where they called the shots, today it appears they are back to square one.

Opposition Getting Weak by the Day

Come 2024, the Opposition, that is, the INDIA bloc, is crumbling, and Prime Minister Modi is on the cusp of a historic third term in office. The leadership deficit in the Congress allows for regional party leaders not to take it seriously. Regional leaders such as Mamata Banerjee, M.K. Stalin, Arvind Kejriwal, Y.S. Jagan Mohan Reddy, have a common antipathy to the Congress. Mamata and Reddy broke away from the Congress to formulate their parties. Each of these parties has managed to attain power by depriving Congress of its vote share, and their party cadre is locked in fierce combat with them in one state or another. The voter is not blind to all these existing elements of contradiction in the INDIA bloc. They cannot claim to be national allies but fight state elections as rivals. After the results of the 2024 Lok Sabha elections, these parties will be back to where they began.

The Era of Coalition Politics Is Over

One thing is for sure—there are fewer chances for the Indian electorate in the immediate future to vote for a *khichdi sarkar*. The Indian voter across state geographies has realized that voting in majority governments is more beneficial to them. This is what can be observed since 2014. The voter today wants focussed, hardworking leaders who walk the talk; they do not acknowledge part-time politicians anymore.

Yet, an effective national-level Opposition is essential for any democratic system.

How Does the Opposition Remain Relevant?

The Opposition's search for a narrative and strategy hangs on a wing and a prayer if it does not take action on the following issues:

Focus on Performance

Prime Minister Modi has made it clear that political parties need to take stock of their political strategies, unlearn their previous understanding of what the voter wants and *change*. They cannot depend on the traditional anti-incumbency phenomenon because since 2014 the Indian voter has displayed a tendency of rewarding work. This is why the prime minister has changed the natural tendency for anti-incumbency to a natural tendency for pro-incumbency.

Be Consistent in Messaging

The way forward for any political party is to understand that they cannot expect the voter to support them if they are being contradictory and inconsistent in their messaging. For example, Congress cannot attract a Hindu voter by aligning with the DMK whose leaders make persistent anti-Sanatan comments and who continue to do so even after being chastised by the Supreme Court. Because of its votebank compulsions, the Congress deemed its association with the DMK of greater importance and could not openly criticize it. It would cost the Congress at the elections, even if its leaders do a temple run during the time of elections because this is inconsistent messaging.

Eschew Minority Appeasement

Political outfits need to understand that they cannot take the majority community's faith and will for granted in elections anymore. The Hindus do not expect any special treatment from the state, but they do expect equal treatment. It is time to shake off the pseudo-secular political practice of taking the

Hindus for granted by not acknowledging their aspirations while giving special treatment to minorities in the name of protection. We saw this peak between 2000 and 2013; the result was 2014.

To reiterate, leaders who wish to remain relevant in Indian polity must practise genuine equality, not pseudo-secular equality.

Avoid Parivad Politics

Leaders need to understand that intentions are as important in public life as work is. Today, the Indian voter wishes to see a strong decision-making leader with clear- and forward-thinking economic goals and a consistent and firm stand on national security. Development and security go hand in hand, they are not mutually exclusive. The Indian voter has slowly moved away from party-driven polity to a leader-driven polity where leaders are seen to drive their parties. Moreover, dynastic or family-based politics undermines the principles of meritocracy leading to the promotion of less qualified candidates solely because of their family ties, which alienates the young Indian voter. In the future, family-based parties will shrink because while the first generation of such parties emerged from social movements or through struggles, the second generation got their position merely through entitlement. This is why they are finding it difficult to expand their parties beyond their traditional boundaries.

Need to Focus on Three Core Elements

Leaders who have emerged from the grassroots will be successful in today's Indian political scenario. This is a natural organic phenomenon because such leaders are sympathetic to the dharmic traditions of the masses. Family-based dynamics or alien ideological parties and leaders will be rejected by the people. The BJP's way of working or ideology will be the focal point of the political narrative in the country in the years to come. It may win or lose some state elections, but the political narrative has been set by Prime Minister Modi and will be looked at through the same ideological lens going ahead. This is why, even though there is a huge intra-competition within the BJP, there is dynamism too because of its ideological patron, the RSS. And, because the prime minister is always providing opportunities to new people. This will remain a challenge for other parties to emulate. This is why the next few decades will see the BJP as the party that will be at the focal point of Indian polity.

The growth of any political party is based on three inherent strengths:

- the presence of a mass leader
- strong organizational set-up
- an ideological footprint

Many parties lack these fundamentals. The BJP is the rarest of rare which has, at this moment, all these factors working for them. When it did not have a mass leader, it had a base vote of 7 crore 80 lakh (2009 figure). When it had a popular leader, it came back in majority and has the ideological fitness that helps it grow in challenging times. Hence, the BJP has grown from a two-seat party to a full majority party in just three to four decades. Whereas every other political party that finds itself in the Opposition is shrinking continuously.

Recognize the Rise of the Non-ideological Voter

Indian polity has attained ideological bipolarity with believers in the dharmic way attaching themselves to the BJP and those who believe in the Nehruvian way of life attaching themselves to the Congress. Whenever they find the Congress flagging, they drift towards other parties like the AAP or the TMC or the Left parties. Mass leaders are important because they can get support from neutral or non-ideological voters.

Prime Minister Modi, with his robust feedback mechanism from the ground, also manages to get votes from non-political voters. This makes him unique, hence his politics cannot be looked from a traditional prism. He is the only leader who has achieved mass support without compromising on ethical standards in public life. He has set a new benchmark for leaders to emulate in the future.

Not To Ignore the Growing Importance of Women And the Elderly

In the years to come, the factors that will drive the political narrative will be nationalistic in character. Any party seeking a mandate must be committed to the people and be conscious of the evolving dynamics. India will also see in the long-term future, a polity with dominant welfare narratives decided by women and the elderly who will form a large chunk of the population. Hence it is no surprise that by 2055, the women's voting percentage will beat the voting percentage of men. Because as Indian women are steadily becoming more educated and wealthier, they are becoming more politically aware.

Align with Urban-centric Politics

As the rural moves increasingly into the urban, it is natural that the focus on urban-centric politics will increase. The political narrative will move from rural first to urban first, with an exponential increase in the aspirations of the Indian voter as the standard of living rises.

Focus on Both Dharma And Development

The year 2014 was the first inflection point in Indian polity post-Independence. Since 1947, the political narrative has been driven from a Nehruvian lens with the essence of looking at India from a non-dharmic prism. To reiterate, Narendra Modi's victory in 2014 reflects the emergence of a new political order, where dharma and development move hand in hand. Most analysts did not catch on and were surprised by the bigger mandate in 2019. Jan Ki Baat, however, predicted this accurately.

Conclusion

In my previous book, I said that only a conscious, committed and nationalist Opposition can take on the BJP in 2019. Today, in the run up to the 2024 Lok Sabha Elections, I say that only a conscious, committed, nationalist and dharmic Opposition can take on the BJP, which is sadly missing. Hence, Narendra Modi will go down in history as the only Indian prime minster to remain unbeaten.

Acknowledgements

Over the last eight years God has given me the opportunity to travel the length and breadth of the country across 400 Lok Sabha constituencies and over one lakh km. I am thankful to the people of Bharat for blessing me with their time and wisdom that has enriched me in this journey, and has helped me evolve as a human being.

I am thankful to my parents, my wife and my sisters who have always supported me in my journey to serve Bharat through all my endeavours. I thank all those who mentored me and guided me with their sagacity in this journey of life.

I am also thankful to my team Jan Ki Baat who meticulously travelled the length and breadth of the country with sincerity. Their efforts in data analysis and behavioural science have helped me predict more than 39 Indian elections accurately.

Last but not the least, the team at Om Books International for publishing this book at such short notice, and Lipika Bhushan and Anshu Dogra for their constant support in writing the book.